THE RAY-WAY

TARP BOOK

How to make a Tarp and Net-Tent, and use them in the wilds

Lightweight shelters for backpackers and hikers, cyclists, sea-kayakers, canoeists, scouts, and anyone else who enjoys camping

by Ray Jardine

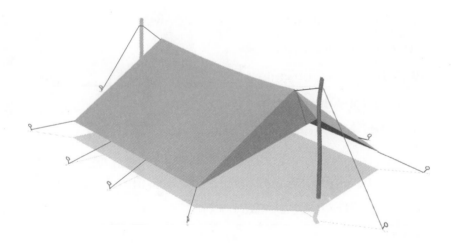

The Ray-Way Tarp Book

How to make a Tarp and Net-Tent, and use them in the wilds

Lightweight shelters for backpackers and hikers, cyclists, sea kayakers, canoeists, scouts, and anyone else who enjoys camping

First Printing. Published in the United States by

AdventureLore Press

P.O. Box 2153, Arizona City, AZ 85223

e-mail: info@AdventureLore.com

www.AdventureLore.com

Library of Congress Control Number: 2003105201

Ray Jardine, The Ray-Way Tarp Book

AdventureLore Press, Arizona City, Arizona

ISBN 0-9632359-5-8

Contents

Dodge DiVall: Making your gear is fool-proof. I've used the tarp on several trips in various weather conditions and it has worked wonderfully. Thank you for sharing your ideas. It will make all my trips more enjoyable.

David J. Miller: I have just returned from a rainy, five day, four night canoe trip in the Oswegatchie Wilderness of New York's Adirondack Park. The area is a beautiful roadless wilderness and there is old growth timber at Griffin Rapids. I camped in my new, self-made, Ray-Way two person tarp with beaks. I am thrilled with the results: the tarp is very dry, spacious, and comfortable. As predicted, I had no problem with water although the people in tents did.

Patrick Wheatley: The sewing projects have changed the way I look at life. Before I started reading Beyond Backpacking I was caught up in the gear buying trap. I have since completed my first tarp, and I am almost finished with the net-tent Beyond sewing and saving money and weight I feel empowered to explore my creative side, a part of me that needs to expand. Sewing has opened a whole new vista on the way I lead my life. It has shown me that I can accomplish anything I set my mind to. Thank you for sending me down my own path.

Introduction

This book is for everyone who enjoys the freedom of camping. The information applies to backpacking and hiking, as well as bicycle touring, river rafting, canoeing, sea kayaking, small sailboat tripping, and most other forms of outdoor recreation that require overnight shelter from the elements.

The most common type of camping shelter is of course the tent. But its popularity is mainly due to its resemblance to a person's home, in miniature. Yet despite its popularity, the tent exhibits a number of problems, usually overlooked but nonetheless real. In this book I describe those problems, and recommend something that I think works better: the tarp.

The use of the tarp dates back to antiquity, when early peoples took shelter under a few animal hides sewn together with sinew, or mats woven of dried plant material. Today we can only imagine these primitive shelters slung over poles lashed between trees, and looking very rustic and woodsy. But we do know that tarps have been around a long while, and for good reason: they are simple and effective.

My experience with the tarp dates back to 1970, when I began using them on summer-long wilderness programs in the Colorado Rockies. That was over three decades ago, and since then I have camped in the wilds more than 2,500 nights. Most of those were in a tent, while about 700 have been under a tarp.

Initially my tarps were quite basic. But because the weather was often severe, with strong wind, heavy rain, and sometimes snowfall, I began improving the design of my tarps, making them lighter, stronger, and more weather-resistant. The design process has been evolutionary, aided by my aerospace engineering background and seasoned with many years of trial-and-error experimentation. The result is the tarp I use today, known as the "ray-way" tarp.

The term "ray-way" is not something I came up with. Rather, it was bequeathed upon my methods and equipment by the lightweight hiking community. The term is in such common use elsewhere that I am borrowing it for use in this book, in places where I wish to differentiate my designs from those of other people.

In this book I describe the more serious problems with tents, and I explain why the ray-way tarp works better in most cases. I show how to use my tarp easily, safely and comfortably in fair weather and foul. And because this tarp is so simple in design and construction, I detail the methods for sewing one together yourself. Those who do not know how to sew may be surprised at how easy it is. And as many first-timers who have constructed these tarps for themselves will attest, the results are well worth the effort.

Also described in this book are the net-tent and poly-tarp. The net-tent is a netting enclosure designed to fit beneath the ray-way tarp for protection from mosquitos and blackflies. The poly-tarp is a generic shelter made of ordinary hardware-store plastic sheeting. I include it here because it is simple yet reasonably effective.

Because of the evolutionary nature of my tarp's design, its every aspect is there for a reason, and anything changed, added or removed will detract from its performance. As such, the information in this book applies only to the ray-way tarp.

In many ways, camping is a means of reestablishing one's bond with the natural world. Lying down to sleep on nature's bed with a tarp overhead, we might hear the wind whispering through the trees, or perhaps the call of a nightingale or an owl. These simple pleasures can lead to a greater appreciation of nature, and a heightened awareness that I and many others, both past and present, refer to as the Connection. Certainly, the tarp facilitates that connection, and this is one of its more important advantages.

This book reflects my findings that the ray-way tarp allows for a simpler, drier and more comfortable and connected approach to wilderness camping. Yet I describe this tarp only as an alternative to the tent. Read the book, study the design, advantages and pitching methods. Then spend a few nights camping beneath a ray-way tarp or a poly-tarp. Only then will you be able to make a more educated and experienced decision about what type of shelter works best for you.

Tarp Evolution: the Poly-Tarp

In my life of outdoor adventure, it seems that nothing has surpassed the simple pleasure of a night spent sleeping in the wilds. I am grateful for these nights, for whether starlit or stormy, challenging or serene, each one has brought me close to nature.

There have been many such nights in my life, beginning with my first camping experiences as a youngster. Back then, my brothers and I would spread our blankets on the lawn behind our home. Never mind that our parents may have been keeping a watchful eye. To us this was freedom and independence; camping at its best.

Then came boyhood trips to the Colorado high country with my father and brothers. Those crisp evenings around the campfire, with the majestic, craggy peaks towering all around. I had my own sleeping bag then, and used a two-person army surplus pup tent made from two pieces of canvas joined along the ridge with buttons. It had neither floor nor mosquito netting, and was more akin to a walled tarp.

In my early twenties I worked as an aerospace engineer, but spent most weekends climbing mountains. That was back in the 1960's, and on many of those outings I slept in a tent sewn from a kit. My down-filled sleeping bag was one I had made from scratch. I was not particularly good at sewing, but I enjoyed working with my hands, and considered the effort well worthwhile in terms of the joy of using my own home-made gear. For I found that it gave me a better sense of presence and belonging in the wilds.

In 1970 I quit my engineering job and applied to teach wilderness courses in the Colorado Rockies. My application was accepted, bolstered perhaps by many years of high-country camping and climbing experience. But imagine my surprise when I showed up for my first summer's orientation and learned that my students and myself would be using—not tents—but tarps. Tarps? The Rockies are infamous for stormy and unpredictable weather, and I wondered how we would manage. Then when

I learned that our tarps would be nothing but ordinary hardware-store 3 mil polyethylene plastic, I was even more taken aback.

The poly-tarp

Logic suggested that these tarps must work, since the instructors and their students had been using them successfully in summers past. I was given a three-minute lesson, and suddenly it all made sense.

What followed were six summers of teaching these classes in Colorado, Oregon and Washington. Typically on day one, myself and eight to twelve college-age students hiked up into the high country, and there we remained for twenty three days of backpacking adventure. Naturally, we encountered all sorts of weather, including strong wind, rain, hail, sleet, and even snow. And not a tent to be seen anywhere among us. Why? Because our tarps worked much better.

Today I refer to these plastic tarps as "poly-tarps," a term I coined in the early 90's. And simple though the poly-tarps were, they offered a wide range of advantages.

Drier

Most important to us, the poly-tarps kept us drier than tents would have, during those times when the weather was persistently wet. This was due to the tarp's superior ventilation. For one or two nights, tents would have served us well enough. But after several days of rain, the moisture trapped in a tent can permeate the sleeping bags and clothing. Day after day the effect can multiply, and if the nights are also cold, as they often were for us, the trapped moisture can sap body heat and ultimately lead to hypothermia. Yet snug in our sleeping bags beneath our well-ventilating tarps, we slept warm and dry.

More reliable

Out in the wilds for weeks at a time, we depended on our shelters. We could not afford the risk of a tent pole buckling in strong wind, or a zipper jamming. When scurrying to make camp in a sudden rain, someone could have stepped on a tent pole or ripped out a zipper. Either could have rendered the tent unserviceable. Our tarps had none of these complexities, so the risks of failure were practically nil.

Stronger

Often during these courses we climbed far above timberline. And sometimes we even camped there, mostly for the added challenge. And challenge we sometimes met, with winds so strong they might have flattened most backpacking tents. But in such conditions we pitched our poly-tarps very low-lying, to reduce the effects of the wind. In extreme wind we placed large rocks along the edges to hold the tarps down and keep them from blowing away. So in effect, the lower we pitched the poly-tarps, the stronger they became.

Economical

Our poly-tarps were far more economical than tents. Each tarp lodged four students and cost only a few dollars. With our limited budgets, this was a feature we appreciated,

Yet despite its low cost, the plastic material proved surprisingly durable. So durable, in fact, that it would last, not just one 23-day course, but an entire summer comprising three such courses. The durability was important because we tended to be hard on gear—mainly due to the boisterous weather and rugged alpine terrain.

Weight savings

For four people, a pair of two-person tents would have weighed eight or ten pounds. A four-person poly-tarp weighs less than two pounds. So in addition to saving money, the poly-tarps saved us packweight.

Simple construction

At the beginning of each summer, I would cut three sheets of polyethylene from a store-bought roll. Each piece measured about 10 feet wide and 14 feet long, enough for a four-person tarp. That was all there was to it. Total construction time: about a minute.

Four Point Plan

On day one at our staging area, we loaded the packs and commenced our long trek into the high country. After hiking maybe five miles that first day, we would stop early and I would explain my Four Point Plan for selecting a suitable camping site. Basically it went like this:

1) Climb high, camp low

Normally we followed the backcountry adage: climb high and camp low. This was because the lower the camp, the warmer the nights and less forceful the wind. Where possible we pitched the tarps in the shelter of trees or rocks. And where the wind was unavoidable, we oriented the tarps sideways to it.

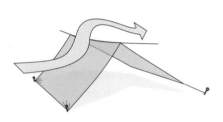

2) Avoid dished ground

I taught my students to avoid any site where the ground was lower than its immediate surroundings. "Dished" is how I described it. Rain can pool in these depressed areas, and can turn them into the equivalent of small ponds.

3) Look up

And of course I advised everyone to check their prospective sites for overhead branches or nearby dead or weak trees that might topple in a storm.

4) Minimize impact

Finally, I emphasized the importance of selecting a site that allows the absolute minimum of impact; one that requires no rearranging of the landscape or damaging of vegetation. And once we had selected a site, I reiterated the benefits of keeping our impact to a minimum so that we could leave the area in its original, natural condition.

Pitching the poly-tarp

To begin pitching their poly-tarps, each four-person group would select a pair of trees. Ideally these two trees would stand about 15 feet apart, to accommodate the tarp's 14-foot length. But if the trees were 20 feet apart, or even 25, they would still suffice.

From these trees the students would string a length of cord, at about chest height. This cord served to support the tarp's ridge, and the students stretched the cord taut to prevent it sagging excessively under the weight and pull of the tarp. Over the ridge line they draped their poly-tarp, A-frame fashion with the material centered on the ridge line, half of it hanging over one side of the line, and half over the other.

The "two trees" method was so easy that it allowed the students to grasp the basic skills of tarp camping in a matter of minutes. Of course, other methods work well, also. Sometimes we would support the tarp from one tree and one stout stick, borrowed from the forest. Or we would omit the trees altogether and use two support sticks. Later in this book I explain all three pitching methods.

At this point I would gather everyone around, and demonstrate the method of tying a line to the corner of the plastic tarp, using a sheet bend or double sheet bend.

The sheet bend

The sheet bend, I explained, is the strongest way to attach a cord to a poly-tarp. Unlike grommets, the sheet bend will not rip out. And because of that, it eliminates the need for additional attachment points along the sides of the poly-tarp.

When learning this knot at home, you could practice with the corner of a bed sheet or towel, in lieu of a tarp.

Tying the sheet bend

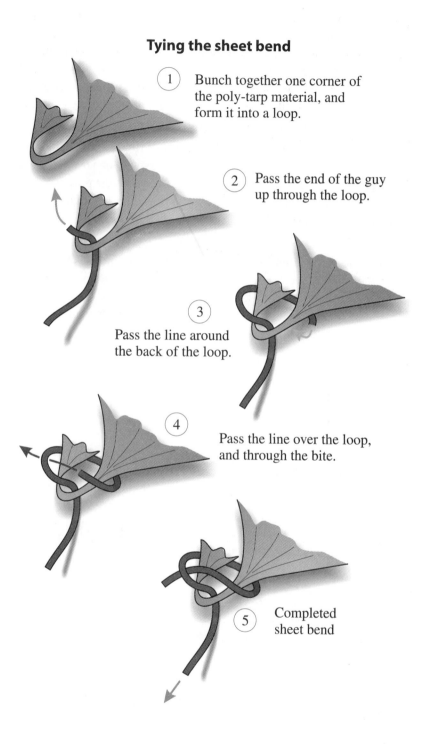

1. Bunch together one corner of the poly-tarp material, and form it into a loop.

2. Pass the end of the guy up through the loop.

3. Pass the line around the back of the loop.

4. Pass the line over the loop, and through the bite.

5. Completed sheet bend

As the group looked on, I would show how to tie the sheet bend. First, I would bunch together one corner of the plastic material, and form it into a loop, as shown here in the diagram. Then I would pass the line up through this loop. After wrapping the line around behind the loop I would pass it over the loop, then beneath the bight of line itself. To finish the knot I would tighten it securely by holding the loop in one hand and pulling one end of the line in a direction away from the loop, then pulling the other end of the line away from the loop.

Double sheet bend

After the students had practiced the sheet bend, I showed them how to tie a double sheet bend. Here, the line simply passes around the loop a second time. The double sheet bend is no stronger, but it tends to stay together better when not loaded, for example as we folded the tarps and loaded them into the backpacks.

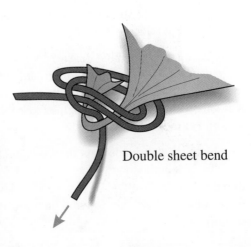

Double sheet bend

At that point the students tied a sheet bend, or a double sheet bend (their choice) to each corner of their tarps.

Consider the weather

Next, I explained that in fine weather they could pitch the tarp higher above the ground, for better ventilation, and in stormy weather spread it wider and closer to the ground, for the best protection. This is a simple matter of raising or lowering the ridge, then adjusting the corner lines.

Anchor securely

At this point I reminded everyone to anchor the lines securely, to prevent the wind from dislodging or blowing their tarps away in an unexpected gust.

The students would then stake out the corners of their poly-tarps. Actually, we did not carry metal tent stakes. Rather, we improvised with sticks, rocks and brush, as described later in this book.

Our poly-tarp camps

With the poly-tarps pitched, the students would crawl beneath them and preen their sleeping areas gently of pinecones and sticks. Gently, meaning they would not root out any vegetation, or sweep away the beneficial pine needles, leaves and underlying decomposed material known as "duff." By leaving this naturally soft bedding in place, they would not need to dig hip holes or do any other excavating, which would tend to damage the landscape. For we always took great care to preserve our impromptu sites in their original pristine condition, so that once we had moved on, we would leave no trace of our presence for anyone to discover.

After gently preening the site, they would spread out their individual groundsheets. These came from the same roll of polyethylene material as the tarps, and were about a foot longer than body length, and about three feet wide. The groundsheets helped keep their foam pads clean and dry, as well as free of tree sap.

Onto their groundsheets they would spread their foam pads. These were body length, about 2 feet wide and 3/8 inch thick. These relatively thin pads worked well because we camped on untrammeled ground, rather than in established campsites, which are typically hard and compacted from overuse.

Greater Connection

The tarps enabled us to remain more in touch with our surroundings. Even while in bed we could see out the open ends, and beneath the sides. This made us feel more in tune with the landscape; with the going and coming of animals, large and small; with the wind whispering in the conifers overhead. I taught my students to appreciate, not the inner cocoon of a tent, but the beauties and activities of nature all around. And with the earth's gentle embrace beneath, our simple, low-tech style encouraged a profound Connection with the natural world.

Zero impact

When breaking camp in the mornings, we would take down the poly-tarps. However, we would not untie the double sheet bends from the plastic material. Once tied, these knots remained in place for the duration of the outing.

With the tarps folded and the backpacks loaded, we would spend a few purposeful minutes restoring the area to its natural condition. This we referred to as "zero-impacting" the site. We picked up any neglected bits of rubbish; returned any rocks that we had used to their original locations; dispersed any sticks we had collected. During my first year or so, the most awkward part was eradicating the remains of the campfire. So we began cooking on stoves, and resorting to campfires only when needing to dry clothing at the end of a long, rainy day.

I recall one such occasion in the Oregon Cascades. We had been hiking in pouring rain for five days and the students were beginning to feel a bit glum. I asked them for their tarps, saying I would meet them a ways further along. Pressing ahead, I reached our pre-arranged location and pitched their tarps—three large ones housing four people each—head height and arranged in a triangle, facing each other. In the center I built a radiating campfire; again something I rarely did, but this was an exceptional circumstance, weather-wise. Each tarp was about eight feet from the fire, so there was little chance of it catching sparks. Before long the students lumbered into camp, and what a look of surprise on their faces when they saw their shelters awaiting them, and encircling the drying campfire.

I can only imagine what that evening would have been like had we been using tents. What could we have done but crawl into the dismal things, and into our dank sleeping bags. What is wrong with building a campfire in front of a tent? In the unlikely event of a tent catching fire, its occupants could be trapped in an inferno. Of course, we could have stood near the campfire in the open rain, but this would have only soaked us more. Either way, what a miserable evening that would have been. But thanks to the tarps the evening was most pleasant, everyone seated beneath their tarps, chatting amicably while drying their clothes, and absorbing the luxurious warmth of the campfire.

A timeless design

Three decades have passed since my participation in those wilderness programs, and all the while I have continued to refine my hiking and camping methods. Yet I still consider the poly-tarp a viable option. Granted, you may never see one featured on an outfitter's showroom floor. The modern gear industry could not reap their huge profits from something so simple and inexpensive. But free of the materialistic bias back then, my students took to the poly-tarp quite easily, and demonstrated its true worth for themselves. Year after year they proved what today's glossy magazines dare not reveal: that this type of tarp works.

Experiences with Tents

After a few years of using a single-person poly-tarp in my wilderness courses, I switched to a similar tarp made of nylon. This I made myself, sewing two lengths of nylon together along the ridge, and sewing attachment loops to the corners and along the sides. This was in 1974, and it was the first step in the ray-way tarp's evolution.

Years later, in the mid 1980's, as Jenny and I were preparing for our first summer-long trek, I sewed together a two-person nylon tarp. Based on how well this type of shelter had worked for me in the past, I thought it might serve us well on this trip.

Yet after studying reams of backpacking "information," (most of which I later realized was more like propaganda) we fell prey to the marketeers' hype. Convinced by the glossy advertising and gear reviews, and by the well-meaning "experts" at the local gear shops, we decided to go with a commercial tent. For after all, neither of us had hiked anything nearly as long as the 2,700-mile Pacific Crest Trail, and we incorrectly came to believe that only the "very best" (most expensive) gear would enable success. And so it was that we settled on a 4 pound, 3-season backpacking tent of the very latest design.

That summer we carried fairly heavy loads—typically 30 or 35 pounds including food and fuel. So when it came time to make camp at day's end, we were usually too tired to enjoy the evenings. About all we wanted was to collapse into the tent.

Most mornings we would awake to find our sleeping bag and clothing damp. The dampness was caused by the tent's inadequate ventilation. Moisture from our breath and evaporation from our skin had accumulated inside the tent, and condensed in our sleeping gear and clothing. This meant that during the day we had to stop and dry things out. We saw other hikers doing the same, and I remember one fellow in particular stopping to chat with us, and matter-of-factly pitching his free-standing tent inside-out, to dry. This build-up of moisture is characteristic of virtually all tents. And while it was merely an inconvenience during the initial weeks of our journey through the arid regions of California, it became more problematic as we progressed further north.

Tent failure

This build-up of moisture inside a tent can sometimes be dangerous. Jenny and I were on the trail in central Oregon later that season when a severe storm moved into the area. It began with several inches of snow—and this was mid-July. Then the snow turned to rain that poured from the sky. We plodded on for half a day, then made an early camp. This was before we had learned to carry umbrellas, so were ill equipped to hike in heavy and prolonged rain. Or to camp in it either, we soon learned.

For the next forty-two hours we remained in the tent, listening to the rain pummeling down while enduring the tent's lack of ventilation. Moisture given off by our breath and bodies condensed on the tent walls, dripped down and was absorbing into the sleeping bag. Sometimes we opened the door for fresh air. This admitted rain, both from above and ricocheting from the ground. When we closed the door, the humidity climbed back to the saturation point, and resumed soaking the tent's interior. Outside, rain rebounded under the fly, drenching the tent's interior walls even further. Braving the elements, I guyed the fly away from the base of the tent to encourage a little more ventilation and to distance the rebounding splash. This helped, but not enough, for every hour our sleeping bag and clothing continued to grow wetter. And as they did, they lost ever more of their ability to keep us warm. Clearly, time was beginning to work against us. Our equipment was inexorably failing, leaving us little choice but to emerge from our so-called "shelter," pack up, make our soggy way out of the mountains, and hitchhike to the nearest town.

Convinced that we needed a more substantial tent that offered better rain protection, we mail-ordered a new one. This of course confined us to the town for several days, waiting for our package. The new tent was heavier, but in such weather we considered it worth the extra weight. So we set off with renewed confidence—until the next heavy rainstorm a few nights later when this new tent exhibited much the same problems.

The Jardine tent awning

That original tent, which had failed us in the heavy Oregon rainstorm, was supposedly state-of-the-art. It had appeared in numerous advertisements in the backpacking and outdoor magazines. It had received lavish praise by the so-called experts in the equipment comparisons and reviews. And it had even received a design award as one of the year's best new products. But our experiences with this tent suggested that this type of advertising is motivated more by paychecks and profit than the actual consumer's welfare.

Preparing for our second PCT hike, in 1991, we made a few modifications to this tent. First, we sewed a short "weather skirt" around the fly's perimeter. This helped alleviate the splash from rain striking the ground near the fly and rebounding onto the body of the tent.

Also we sewed a simple awning to the tent fly, extending over its doorway. The awning improved the tent, for during the second PCT hike it allowed us to keep the door fully open in all sorts of weather, even in the heaviest of rain. The open doorway helped ventilate the interior, and this reduced, but not eliminated, the trapped moisture. And as a bonus the awning sheltered our backpacks.

To compensate for the awning's added weight, while preparing for our third trip—a thru-hike of the Continental Divide Trail—I cut away the tent's vestibule. This created a huge open doorway, covered by the awning. On this trip we always tried to pitch the tent with its foot pointing toward the wind, to protect the open doorway. Where this was not possible, due to ground slope usually, we sometimes lowered the awning so that its front edge was close to the ground. So in effect, the awning served as a door when necessary. Yet it hardly ever was necessary. In fact, even during our trek of the Appalachian Trail the following year, we rarely needed to lower the awning to keep out the rain.

In the Sewing chapter of Beyond Backpacking I describe how to make such an awning.

Objectivity regained

During those four thru-hikes we considered the tent essential. Writing this now, years later, this belief seems unfounded. But here is why I think we had become dependent on tents:

It began with the marketeers hype. The glossy magazines—funded by advertisers—had convinced us to believe that a tent was the ultimate in portable shelters. Largely this belief was fear based. The marketeers repeatedly reminded us of the ravages of nature, then assured us that their tents would shelter us comfortably. Also, the magazines showed beautiful people enjoying life in the wilds, alongside their tents. Subconsciously, this type of messaging sinks in. None of us is immune to it.

The more Jenny and I had gone along with the typical magazine ballyhoo, the deeper our belief in tents. Moreover, as our mega-hikes began to unfold, we grew ever more familiar with the routine of pitching the tent and crawling inside. The tent and its perceived security became synonymous with a good night's rest at the end of a long day on the trail. So not only was the tent our "security," it was also our reward.

For many of these same reasons, I think most campers rely on tents. Simply put, the more experienced a person is with tents, the more accustomed to them and actually dependent on them. And therefore the less open to alternatives.

And here is the strange part: The beliefs that Jenny and I held for tents, fostered by the advertising industry and by the sight of the other hikers and campers using tents, were so strong that they blinded us to the tent's disadvantages. Our tents were working poorly for us, yet we considered it, not a shortcoming of the tents, but a simple fact of backpacking—like the proverbial price one must pay to reap the rewards.

Nearly 12,000 miles of hiking and more than 500 nights. That is how long it took us to regain objectivity. The tents were not working well for us. In the morning our clothing and bedding were damp. Every day we had to air out the quilt and dry the inside of the tent. Every night the condensation and humidity inside the tent returned. In mild weather the absorbed moisture and loss of insulation was inconvenient. In stormy, alpine weather it was dangerous. The magazines were telling us that the more severe the weather, the more we needed a heavy-duty backpacking tent. But our experiences were telling us the exact opposite: that a tent is ineffective in any kind of weather.

In addition, at close to four pounds, the tents we carried were heavy and bulky. As we accumulated those hundreds and thousands of trail miles, we realized ever more clearly the need to reduce packweight. We were beginning to see how unnecessary weight on our backs reduced our mileage, increased our fatigue, and made us more susceptible to stress injuries.

So while preparing for our fifth mega-hike—the PCT southbound in 1994—we determined to slash packweight. Naturally, the 4-pound tent became an obvious target. Thinking back to our 500 nights in a tent, we

Our thru-hiking with tents			
1987	PCT	2,500 mi.	4 months, 18 days
1991	PCT	2,700 mi.	4 months, 3 days
1992	CDT	2,500 mi.	3 months, 21 days
1993	AT	2,100 mi.	2 months, 28 days
Total		9,800 mi.	14.5 months
Plus 4 pre-season training		2,000 mi.	100 nights
Total hiked in tent mode		11,800 mi.	
Total nights in a tent			**500**

tried to remember one of those nights where a tarp would not have worked. We could not think of a single one. But we certainly could think of a great many nights where a tarp would have worked better than a tent.

So at long last we relinquished our dependence on tents and switched to a two-person tarp.

Our return to the tarp

The tarp we decided to carry on our fifth thru-hike was the same one I had sewn in advance of our 1987 hike. Finally, seven years later, I had regained my confidence in this simple, lightweight shelter. Now I realized it would work well on an extended journey. And indeed, during the ensuing 2,700 trail miles we used this tarp with excellent results. Beneath it we slept much drier, without the trapped moisture typical with tents. And it might be true that the added ventilation of a tarp made more oxygen available to the lungs. For we slept better, and typically in the mornings awoke feeling more refreshed.

The tarp we used on this PCT southbound journey was simple in design. Rectangular in shape, it was made from two pieces of urethane-coated nylon sewn together lengthwise along its ridge seam. It had a small loop of nylon webbing sewn into each end of the ridge, as attachment points. It had similar webbing loops sewn to each of the four corners, and two additional loops sewn to each side, for the guys. This tarp did not have lifters, or beaks (described shortly).

Since we were hiking the PCT southbound this time, and since we began early in the North Cascade's hiking season, we trudged through nearly 300 miles of snow through Washington. But not once did we sleep on snow, for we always found at least a small bare patch of ground to camp on. So the tarp worked very well for us.

After the initial 700 trail miles we detoured to our home in central Oregon for a few days. And it was there that we added a useful feature that I call "lifters." These raise the roof in key areas, and increase the tarp's sheltered living space. (More about lifters in the next chapter.) Thus configured, this tarp accompanied us on the remaining 2,000 miles to the Mexican Border.

It was during these two months of hiking with this tarp that I conceived of the beaks, or drooped ends, as a way to help shelter the interior living space. This is when the variable geometry idea took shape; that is, the stormier the weather, the lower the tarp pitch, and the more the beaks angle downwards to help shelter the occupants. In subsequent years we sewed together a number of prototypes, and tested and proved them on numerous outings. Thus, the ray-way tarp was born.

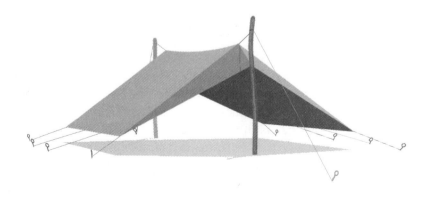

The Tarp Advantage

The ray-way tarp is intended for normal three-season use, in moderate climes. When used according to the instructions in this book, I think it outperforms a modern backpacking tent in a number of important ways.

Warmth: tarp and tent compared

The tarp is open at each end, ventilating its interior in a way that far surpasses that of any tent. Too much ventilation on a windy day, one might imagine, thinking of that cozy, enclosed tent. But in my experience, a properly pitched ray-way tarp blocks the wind just as effectively, if not more so. How? We orient the tarp broadside to the wind, and lower its windward edge to the ground if necessary. And we pitch it low-lying in moderate to strong wind, thus bringing the beaks into play.

Whether the wind is strong or non-existent, the superior ventilation of the ray-way tarp makes for drier living quarters. And drier is warmer. To understand how this works, let's look at a few details.

Moisture buildup inside a tent

During the night we each give off several pounds of water, in the form of vapor. Some is lost with each exhalation, and the remainder evaporates from our skin. If we are sleeping beneath a tarp, this vapor wafts away. But if in a tent, much of the vapor accumulates.

What about the open gap below the tent fly? Doesn't it ventilate the tent's interior, allowing the vapor to escape? No. The vapor is buoyant, warmed by body heat. So it rises, only to be contained by the tent's ceiling and walls. A hot air balloon is wide open at the bottom, and for the same reason its opening does nothing to ventilate the balloon's interior. Despite various claims that certain tents ventilate well, in my experience the only time they do is in gale-force winds.

Inside a tent, much of the vapor given off by our breath and skin has nowhere to go, so it accumulates in the quilt or sleeping bag, and condenses into moisture. Were we to weigh the sleeping bag when perfectly dry, say after airing it for an hour in the bright sun, and weigh it again after a night in the tent, it would be about two pounds heavier.

This entrapped moisture degrades the sleeping bag's ability to insulate. To compensate, the sleeping bag must be extra thick, so that it will still keep us warm.

This extra thickness adds weight and bulk in the backpack. And of course the two pounds of moisture certainly adds to packweight also. Such are the hidden costs of that cozy tent.

In mild weather, the tent camper dutifully "airs out" the sleeping bag every day. Twenty or thirty minutes in the bright sun will remove the accumulated moisture, returning the bag to a serviceable condition for use the following night. However, if the weather is persistently wet, then the bag cannot be aired. And if used again the following night it will accumulate even more dampness, reducing its insulating value even further. Several nights of this and the bag will have lost most of its ability to keep the person warm.

The problem is not with the quilt or sleeping bag, but the tent. However, the person may not realize this, so he or she may become disenchanted with camping, or might resolve to buy a new sleeping bag with a lower-temperature rating, of course adding even more weight and bulk to the load.

Benefits of superior ventilation

The ray-way tarp is open at each end. This prevents the vapor from accumulating, keeping the quilt or sleeping bag much drier during the night and functioning at its best.

All well and good; but still you might wonder how a tarp could be as warm as a tent when a cold wind is blowing.

Actually, a correctly pitched ray-way tarp will block the wind, leaving only a minor breeze wafting through its interior, even in a storm. This wafting breeze plays over the quilt or sleeping bag, and is extremely beneficial in keeping you warm, even if the air itself is cold. Here is why:

As you lie there snugly in your quilt or sleeping bag, the quilt or bag blocks the breeze and prevents it from reaching your skin. The breeze cannot penetrate the insulation more than a fraction of an inch. But as it plays over the surface of the quilt or bag, it draws away the moisture the insulation contains. And it is this extra drying effect that enables the quilt or sleeping bag to function at its best, and keep you warm.

This is true on a dry night and a wet one. And it is especially applicable in regions of high humidity. In fact, the ray-way tarp ventilates so well that it enables the use of goose down insulation, for those who might prefer it over synthetic. And the tarp obviates any benefits of a vapor-barrier system, promoted by some companies largely to overcome the inadequate ventilation of their tents. At least in normal three-season conditions, which is the context of these discussions.

Shortcomings of tent in rain

Visit your local backpacking shop and examine the tents pitched on the showroom floor. While looking at a particular model, ask yourself this: with the tent's door wide open, would rain fall directly into its interior? Or perhaps would rain run or drip into the open doorway? Remarkable as it may seem, in light of the industry's supposed sophistication, most tents cannot pass this simple test.

Why is this test important? Due to the tent's lack of adequate ventilation, you will rarely if ever keep its door closed. Even during an extended period of rain, a wide-open door will help ventilate the interior and reduce the moisture buildup in your clothing and sleeping gear. An open door does not eliminate the moisture buildup, but a closed one multiplies this buildup many times over.

If you must keep the door closed in order to block the rain, then the trapped moisture will permeate your clothing and quilt or sleeping bag, and the ambient chill may even begin to plunge you into a survival-type situation. Such an occurrence would not be a weather attack, but a tent failure.

Problems with pitching a tent in rain

Ironically, most tents are not designed to be pitched in the rain. So the task can be, at best, problematic. While fully exposed to the rain, you quickly and not-too-thoroughly preen the site of any sticks, pinecones and obvious rocks that might puncture the floor. Then you pull the tent poles from your pack, while trying to keep the rest of the tent out of the rain. You snap the poles together hastily and set them aside. Then you lay out your groundsheet, which starts acting as a rain catcher, and quickly you withdraw your tent from its stowbag and spread it, floor-side down, over the now-wet groundsheet. This of course traps the wetness between the floor and groundsheet. And since the body of the tent is now exposed to the rain, it is rapidly getting wet. You fumble with the poles, now wet and slippery, and finally you manage to erect the tent and hurriedly cast its waterproof fly over it.

Of course, you could have tried to cover the tent with its fly before erecting the tent, but in most cases that would have caused even more fumbling.

Either way, you attach the fly to the tent, and stake out its vestibule— provided the fly has a vestibule. And if so, then you stuff your wet backpack beneath it. Due to the fluster of scurrying about, you are now wet with condensation inside your rain jacket. You remove the jacket, place it in the vestibule atop your backpack where neither can possibly dry. Then at long last you crawl into the decidedly wet tent. Not to be discouraged, you mop the tent's interior with a hand towel, wringing it out the front door as necessary. And soon your abode is... at least tolerable.

Having settled into the tent, you may long for a cooked meal, or at least a reviving hot drink. However, for safety's sake you cannot use your stove inside the tent, tempting though that might be. Fumes could accumulate and asphyxiate you. Equally dangerous, the stove could accidentally catch your sleeping bag, clothing or the tent itself on fire.

And too, stoves that burn hydrocarbons (gasoline or petrol, propane or gas, alcohol or spirits) give off water vapor as a byproduct of combustion. This moisture would accumulate inside the tent, along with the poisonous fumes.

You could reach out the doorway and cook in the vestibule, only hoping that the carbon monoxide does not waft into the tent and accumulate. Except that your backpack is probably occupying the vestibule. Maybe you could shove the pack out into the rain, and ignite the stove in the vestibule, taking your chances with the fumes.

For safety's sake, let's say you decide to venture out into the pouring rain, and perhaps crouch beneath the partial shelter of a tree. And there you sit, hunkered over a sputtering stove for what scant warmth it provides, soaking wet and becoming more miserably chilled all the time.

This is the modern approach to suffering, and I doubt whether the Cro-Magnons lived as miserably.

Pitching a tarp in rain

Pitching a ray-way tarp in the pouring rain is quite straightforward. You could even shelter yourself with an umbrella in the process. Where the job requires both hands, simply rest the umbrella over the top of you.

With the tarp properly pitched and well anchored, you set your backpack under it, and crawl beneath the tarp yourself. Gently, you preen your bedding area of any sticks, pinecones, and small rocks—while fully sheltered from the rain. Spreading your groundsheet, dry side up, you sit or lie on it while removing your wet clothes and quickly donning dry ones. Then you pull your quilt or bag from its stowbag and place it over you for warmth. Welcome to a warm and dry abode.

A heavy downpour can rebound from the ground and splatter a few inches into the tarp's interior. Because the tarp is quite spacious, this splatter does not reach you or your gear. And unlike a tent where the splatter often soaks the fabric, beneath a tarp the water either evaporates or is absorbed into the ground.

Should the day's clothing be sopping wet, you could wring it out and hang it from the clothesline strung lengthwise along the tarp's underside.

Thanks to its superior ventilation, the ray-way tarp is unlikely to collect stove fumes to any dangerous level, at least when pitched properly. So it affords the luxury of a hot beverage or cooked meal from the warmth and comfort of your quilt or sleeping bag. Cooking under this tarp is reasonably safe, (when not in bear country, for the odors of cooking are powerful attractants) as long as you follow a few common-sense precautions. Keep the flames well away from the tarp, your clothing and sleeping gear. And keep the stove well away from yourself, to avoid an accidental scalding. Place the stove beside the groundsheet, not on it; this will help avoid an upset.

Striking camp in the rain

The unpleasant scenario for pitching a tent in the rain essentially repeats itself in reverse as you break camp. That is, everything is again exposed to the pouring rain, piece at a time, and re-soaked. Not so with a tarp.

Comfortably beneath the tarp, you stuff your quilt into its bag, remove your sleeping garments and place them in their waterproof stowbag, and don the previous day's damp ones. Bracing, yes, but they will soon warm, once you get moving. Still beneath the shelter of the tarp, you now load your backpack, everything but the tarp and umbrella. Umbrella in hand, you emerge from beneath the tarp, and dismantle the tarp. Giving it a few shakes, you stuff it into an external mesh pocket of your backpack, or into its waterproof stowbag and then into your backpack.

If the rain subsides during the day, you can spread the wet tarp to dry. Even if the sun is not shining directly, the tarp will normally dry fairly well if you drape it over brush, or lay it on bare or rocky ground that faces generally toward the sun. But if the rain is persistent, preventing you from drying the tarp, its wetness will not affect its performance the following evening.

Strength: tarp and tent compared

The ray-way tarp is an integration of straight lines and triangles, all in tension. It has no weakness of curved poles in compression, which is one reason it is stronger than a tent. And thanks to its all-tension geometry, it can be constructed of thinner, lighter, and more packable materials.

Speaking of tent poles, one breaking in a strong wind could suddenly render a tent unserviceable. In other words, in conditions so severe that your life depends on your tent, this is when the tent is most likely to fail you. Not so with a tarp. Should a tarp support-stick break, you simply replace it with a stronger one found nearby in the woods. If such a stick is unavailable, then the tarp will still shelter you nicely with only one end elevated.

Variable Geometry Aerodynamics

A tent's shape is fixed. You cannot lower it to reduce the effects of a strong wind. Why is this a disadvantage? When the wind speed doubles, its force against a tent does not merely double, it quadruples. By the laws of physics, the wind's force increases by the square of its speed. This is why a storm can place such enormous strain on a tent and its poles; enough to blow the tent away or crumple it into a heap. My experience has certainly borne this out, with many tent poles broken during storms.

But suppose you are using a tarp. It could be a poly-tarp or a ray-way tarp. When the wind speed doubles, you simply lower the tarp, making it more aerodynamic. This all but eliminates the wind strain.

Weight comparison

The tents that Jenny and I carried on our initial four thru-hikes were state of the art backpacking models. They each weighed about 4 pounds. The home-made, two-person tarp we used on our fifth hike weighed 1¾ pounds. And the two-person ray-way tarp described in the sewing section of this book weighs about 1 pound.

A sense of Connection

So in effect we have reduced the shelter's weight and bulk by three fourths, while essentially doubling its interior living space. We have eliminated the risk of broken tent poles or zippers. We have introduced the all-important element of ventilation, which goes a long ways in keeping us drier, warmer and more comfortable. But of all the ray-way tarp's finest features, it enables a better Connection with our natural surroundings.

A tent can provide a false sense of security. Its walls encourage its occupants to ignore what might be happening outside, and essentially switch off their senses. But tent walls are no barrier to any kind of real threat, should one arise. Security comes not from thin nylon walls, but from remaining alert to any unusual sounds, and watching and actually reacting if necessary. So too, beneath the tarp you can stay more attuned with nature. The night is as full of wonders as the day, so why barricade yourself inside a tent and spend the starry hours in oblivion? You can do that at home, inside your house.

Sheltered beneath a tarp you can experience a closeness to nature. Lying comfortably in your bedding, you will know the feeling of the cool air playing across your face, the rich, green and earthy aromas, and the subtle creaks and chirps and rustlings of nature. You can reach beyond your groundsheet and run your fingers through the pine needles or soft forest duff. It is this kind of intimacy, this Connection with the natural world, that I like most about the tarp.

Features and their Applications

My goal with this tarp has been to keep it simple and lightweight, yet imminently functional. This chapter describes its key features, and explains their applications.

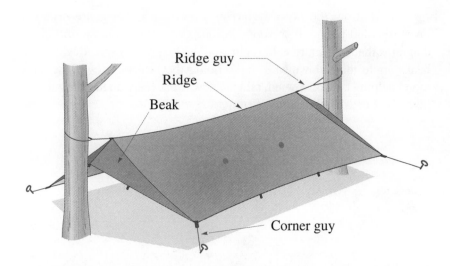

Configuration 1: fine weather

The illustration shows the ray-way tarp in its basic form, pitched between two trees. This configuration is very quick to pitch, since it requires only four stakes or other fastening objects.

The tarp's apex, running end to end, is called the "ridge." Tied to each end of the ridge is a ridge "guy." My dictionary defines the word guy as "a line attached to something to steady or secure it."

One ridge guy is attached to each tree. Additionally, four corner guys lead to ground stakes, spreading the tarp horizontally.

The ridge is actually a sewn seam extending the length of the tarp. This seam joins the two halves, or panels, of material. The seam is necessary for two reasons. One, the material, as it comes from the factory, is not usually wide enough to extend the full width of the tarp. So we sew two lengths together. And two, the ridge seam carries much of the stress between the two ridge guys. These guys pull the tarp in opposing directions, tug-of-war fashion. Thus, the ridge seam is a structural member. Were this seam absent, the tarp would distort in strong wind.

Because the ridge seam consists of several layers of nylon material, and because this material stretches when loaded, the ridge "gives" somewhat when the tarp is hit by a gust of wind. Also, because the ridge is in tension, and because the ridge seam comprises several layers of fabric, the fabric itself can be quite thin without compromising the tarp's overall strength.

In addition, the ray-way tarp has the beaks. These are my own invention, and intend to serve a specific purpose. Note in the following diagrams that as the tarp is lowered, and the two halves spread wider, the beaks angle more downward. In so doing the beaks close off the ends more, helping block the wind, rain or snow. But even with the tarp pitched higher the beaks help shelter the interior.

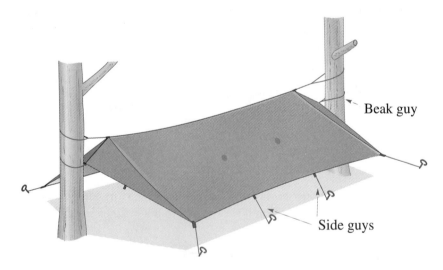

Beak guy

Side guys

Configuration 2: changeable weather

As the weather grows a little more uncertain we can bring a few of the ray-way tarp's other features into play.

This figure shows the same tarp, pitched between the same two trees, but with the addition of side guys. These are not structural in most cases; they merely help support and stabilize the tarp's edges.

Also shown is a pair of beak guys. These guys support only the beaks, not the tarp itself. As such, they are tied only lightly.

Configuration 3: Storm conditions

In strong wind we pitch the tarp lower. This of course reduces headroom, so to help compensate I added a set of "lifters," shown here. The lifters raise the roof on either side, effectively increasing headroom without the need to pitch the tarp higher. This gives more sheltered living space in a storm, at no cost in floor area. (Raising the ridge reduces the floor area by angling the roof steeper and reducing the spread of the sides.) The lifters also help stabilize and support the central roof area on both sides of the tarp in wind, heavy rain and snowfall.

The lifters consist of reinforcement patches sewn to the tarp, two patches on each side, and lifter lines attached to these patches. The lifter lines are tensioned very lightly, only enough to create sufficient headroom without distorting the pitch. They are tied to overhead branches, where available, or to separate support sticks, then angle down to stakes. Ideally these sticks are positioned only about an inch from the tarp, to create the best upward direction for the lift. The lifter sticks need not be stout, again because they are lightly weighted.

Like the side guys, the lifters are a desirable feature, but they are not a necessary part of the tarp's overall strength or performance.

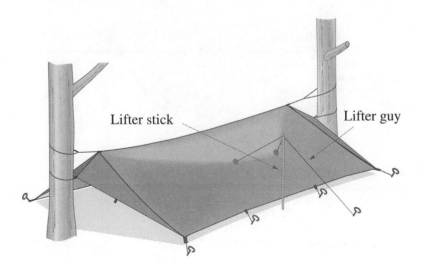

Lifter stick

Lifter guy

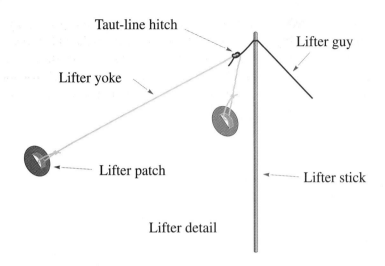

Taut-line hitch

Lifter guy

Lifter yoke

Lifter patch

Lifter stick

Lifter detail

The more detailed illustrations, shown here, may give a better idea of how the lifters work. The lifter line is in two segments, or pieces—a "yoke" and a "guy." One end of the yoke attaches to one reinforcement patch. The other end of the yoke attaches to the other reinforcement patch. One end of the guy attaches to the yoke with a taut-line hitch. From there, the guy leads up to the support stick, wraps around it twice, then angles down to the stake.

Were the guy actually tied to the yoke, it would not be adjustable, side to side. So when pulling from a branch that is off to one side, the

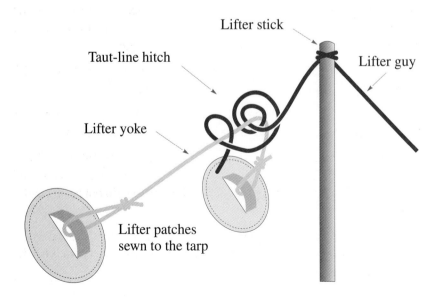

Lifter stick

Taut-line hitch

Lifter guy

Lifter yoke

Lifter patches
sewn to the tarp

force would direct to the tarp's opposite reinforcement patch only. Or were the guy merely looped through the yoke, it would slide too easily, and pull on the nearby reinforcement pad only. But by tying the guy to the yoke with a taut-line hitch, described later, we create enough friction to allow adjustment, side to side, while loading both reinforcement patches more or less equally.

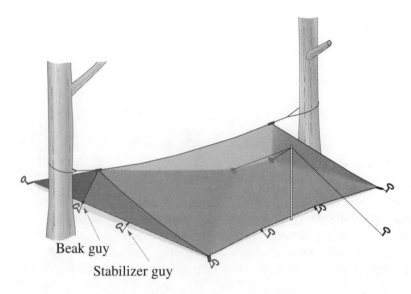

Beak guy

Stabilizer guy

Configuration 4: in gale-force wind

Should the wind start blowing a gale, we can spread the tarp wide and lower it nearly to the ground. In this case we would tension the corner and side guys more, and we might add beak stabilizer guys.

The beak stabilizer guys support the beaks mid-panel. And as with the side guys, they help anchor the tarp in position.

When the tarp is pitched very low-lying, the beak guys are tied, not to the support trees, but to separate stakes or other anchor points.

This fourth configuration will withstand very powerful wind. Most of us will rarely, if ever, encounter such wind, meaning that we would very seldom use beak stabilizer guys. So of course we do not permanently fit them to the tarp.

Note in the illustrations that the lower we pitch the tarp, the closer we tie the corner and side stakes to the tarp, essentially shortening the guys. This adds stability in strong wind.

Note also that when pitching the tarp very low lying, we avoid pitching it so low that it contacts the quilt or sleeping bag. This would restrict the needed ventilation, and would likely soak the quilt or bag with condensation.

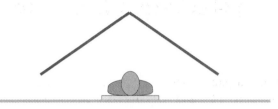

Tarp pitched high in fine weather

Tarp pitched low in stormy weather

Clothesline

The ray-way tarp has a clothesline strung the length of its ridge, on the tarp's underside. This line is quite thin, to save a bit of weight, but it can be very useful for hanging damp socks and shirt, or wet clothes from laundering or rain.

The ray-way tarp is simple in design, lightweight, and very functional. As such, it has no need of the usual plethora of complicated features intended to bolster appearance in catalogs and magazines. It works more in harmony with the natural world, rather than trying to stand up against it. A well-pitched ray-way tarp with its clean, taut shape and angled beaks has the look of simplicity and strength. And even though made of modern fabrics, in the right colors it blends well with the natural environment and looks at home there.

In the following chapter we look at the importance of careful campsite selection for a comfortable and secure night's rest beneath a tarp.

Selecting a Tarp Site

The tarp is not a pitch-anywhere type shelter. But neither is a tent. For example, someone who unwisely pitches a tent in a dry streambed could be washed away in an unexpected deluge. Or suppose someone pitches a tent in an established campground, not noticing the ground at that particular site is dished. An unexpected rain could flood the site. Or suppose someone pitches a tent on a high ridge, fully exposed to the elements. During the night the wind could increase to a howling gale and break the tent poles.

Regardless of the type of shelter, then, site selection is important.

The Four Point Plan

When selecting a tarp site, keep in mind my Four Point Plan:

- Climb high, camp low

- Avoid dished ground

- Look up

- Minimize impact

Let's consider these in some detail.

1) Climb high, camp low

High, exposed areas tend to amplify blustery weather. You can usually eliminate, or at least greatly reduce, weather-related adversities by descending from the stormy heights and camping in a lower and more protected area.

To illustrate the effectiveness of this principle, let me relate a story from our trek of the Continental Divide Trail. Jenny and I met another long-distance hiker in the remote mountains of western Montana. He was hiking north, and we south. The day was late, and after our pleasant conversation the fellow resumed his ascent of the mountain that we had just come down, and we continued our descent. A short ways farther we made a comfortable camp nestled in the pines, and there we enjoyed a very pleasant evening. The highlight was a pair of owls flying round the tent and alighting on a branch just a few yards from our open doorway. In the morning we awoke to find the mountain enveloped in cloud, and we thought of the fellow, who said he intended to camp up there. Months later he sent us a few pages photocopied from his journal, describing a harrowing night on the summit, hanging on to his tent in a savage storm. Our camp and his were only half a mile apart, but ours was protected snugly in a vale, while his was fully exposed to the elements.

Sometimes a long descent from the stormy heights will require an equally long ascent the following day, to regain the route. In stormy weather, count it worth the cost. In the snowbound North Cascades Jenny and I were hiking the PCT southbound when a storm moved into the area. We trudged through blowing snow all afternoon, but eventually the fog and driving spindrift completely obscured the way ahead. So we descended 1½ miles downhill, looking for a protected place to pitch our tarp in the lee of trees, brush, logs or rocks. And indeed, we found a lovely area of snow-free ground protected in a grove of fir and larch. By next morning the storm was lessening, so we climbed back up to our turn-around point, and continued safely on our way.

If the weather is deteriorating and you are searching for the warmest place to pitch your tarp, be aware of any katabatic areas. In Beyond Backpacking I describe the phenomenon in some detail. To summarize: katabatic cooling often takes place in the evenings and at night, when cold, mountain air flows down the drainages and pools in the valleys. The reason it flows and pools is that it is much colder than the ambient air, and therefore heavier. So it behaves almost like water. When descending from the high mountain heights into a valley, then, consider stopping short of the actual valley floor. One or two hundred feet above will usually keep you out of the katabatic "lake." Also, for the warmest night try to stay at least the same distance above a river or streambed.

2) Avoid dished ground

Dished ground is that which is depressed somewhat below its surroundings.

Most sites in established campgrounds are dished. Why? Because they are compacted from so much use. Year after year, decade after decade, people have been walking on them, sitting and lying on them. And occasionally so have their pack animals: horses, mules and llamas. In many cases cars, even heavy maintenance trucks, have driven over these sites. One reason these areas are usually devoid of vegetation is the trampling. Another is that the plants and seedlings have suffocated from the compacted soil's loss of porosity.

Compacted sites are not nearly as comfortable to sleep on, typically requiring a thick foam pad. And during a storm they may collect rain and sometimes become, quite literally, ponds.

So if visiting an established campground, chose your site carefully. Or better yet, avoid established campgrounds altogether, and pitch your tarp in a natural, untrammeled area miles away.

When looking in a natural area for a place to pitch your tarp, imagine what the terrain might look like in a deluge. Water would of course run downhill and pool in the dished areas. Now dry, those dished areas might seem quite appealing with their level surface and lack of foliage in an otherwise densely vegetated area. But the pooling of heavy rain might have swamped any vegetation trying to grow there. And it could swamp anyone who camps there also.

Instead, look for ground that is somewhat elevated above its surroundings, and that slopes gently away on all sides. That way, as rain runs off your shelter, it will course away from your site rather than pool near it or drain back into it.

So use judgment, and think ahead.

3) Look up

Whether in a natural area, or an established campground, be sure to check your potential tarp site for any large, dead branches overhead, or nearby trees that are leaning or possibly weak.

This type of danger is much more common than campers tend to imagine, even in established campgrounds. So again think "what if" and select your site accordingly.

Sometimes, if a branch or leaning tree is weak in appearance, and not too large, and there are no other campers nearby, you might try putting your weight against it. If it won't budge, and if the weather seems stable, your prospective site is probably safe from this object. Otherwise, choose another site.

When deciding where to camp, prudence is in order, but outright fear of every branch or tree that could come down in a once-in-a-century storm is not. The entire forest could topple, and many of us have seen swaths of tangled timber laid flat by a microburst. But such powerful winds are so rare they hardly merit our worry. So we exercise judgment as best we can, taking every reasonable precaution, then we relax and enjoy the evening's camp.

4) Minimize impact

When selecting a site, think about the ecological impact your presence there may have.

Is the site particularly attractive except for a few saplings growing where you would like pitch your tarp, but that you could easily rip out? Give those trees a chance, and look elsewhere for a different site.

Is your prospective site close to a popular trail, and would you create a camp-sized crush in the wildflowers or other delicate vegetation? Think of the impact in the eyes of your fellow outdoor enthusiasts. Give that site a miss; wander well away from the trail and look for a less vegetated place to camp.

The examples are many, but the basic concept holds true. Choose a site that will require the minimum of impact. This concept is especially important along highly popular footpaths and canoe routes.

In my experience, the tarp often reduces and sometimes even eliminates our impact on vegetation by suspending over it rather than crushing it as the floor of a tent would. Many times Jenny and I have shared our living space with saplings, bushes or flowers. And quite often the tarp has fit in an area where a tent would not, by allowing tree branches or brush to extend into its interior.

Sloped ground

When looking for a place to pitch your tarp, you may not be able to find ground that is significantly raised above its surroundings. Often, taking the time to look in a completely different area will yield results. Finding the best site sometimes requires a bit of extra legwork.

If the entire region is relatively flat, look for ground that is sloped. Rain cannot pool on sloped ground, and only in the heaviest of rain will it actually course downhill. Usually it soaks into the earth.

You might not imagine that you could sleep comfortably on sloped ground, but there is a way that works very well.

Sleeping with your head uphill and your feet downhill is not the answer. Gravity would pool the blood into your legs and feet, and so restrict circulation. And your body relies on good circulation for recuperation from the day's activities.

Sleeping laterally on the slope, parallel with it, is not the answer either; for you would likely spend much of the night resisting the tendency to roll downhill.

Instead, sleep with the feet oriented uphill. This eliminates blood pooling in the lower extremities, and it even draws the day's swelling from them. This is especially good therapy for the hiker's legs and feet.

How steep is too steep? I have found it best not to rule out a sloped site until I have checked it by feel, actually lying on it. Sometimes ground that appears too steep will actually feel acceptable. Jenny and I joke that if we awaken the following morning and find that we have slid out from under the tarp, the slope was a little too steep.

On the PCT in 1994, sharing the tarp site with a hemlock.

Methods of Pitching

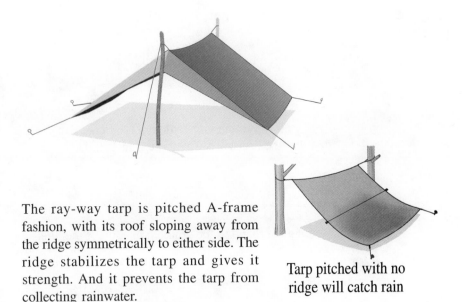

The ray-way tarp is pitched A-frame fashion, with its roof sloping away from the ridge symmetrically to either side. The ridge stabilizes the tarp and gives it strength. And it prevents the tarp from collecting rainwater.

Tarp pitched with no ridge will catch rain

The tarp has three pitching modes:

• Between two trees

• Between one tree and one support stick

• Between two support sticks

Attaching a guy to the tarp

Sewn to the underside of the tarp at its edge are small loops of nylon webbing called "pull loops." The guys attach to these loops.

The best knot for attaching a guy to its pull loop is the overhand on a bight. This knot will not work free over time, as bowlines and other types would tend to do.

Tying an overhand on a bight

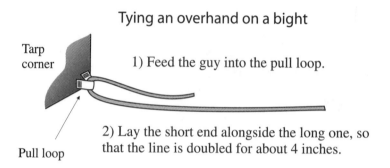

Tarp corner

1) Feed the guy into the pull loop.

2) Lay the short end alongside the long one, so that the line is doubled for about 4 inches.

Pull loop

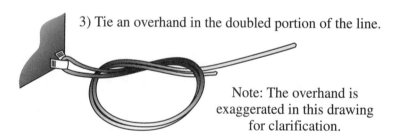

3) Tie an overhand in the doubled portion of the line.

Note: The overhand is exaggerated in this drawing for clarification.

4) While tightening the knot, work it toward the pull loop.

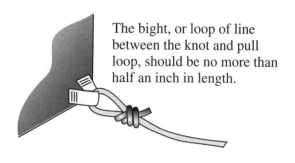

The bight, or loop of line between the knot and pull loop, should be no more than half an inch in length.

All guys are tied to the tarp only once, when the tarp is new. They remain in place essentially for the life of the tarp. (With the exception of the beak stabilizer guys.)

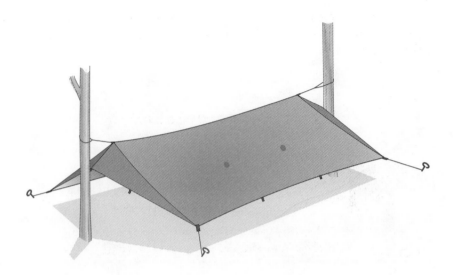

Pitching the tarp between two trees

Where trees are available, the two-tree method is often the easiest way to pitch the tarp.

When selecting your tarp site, look for two trees about a tarp's length apart, and which offer accommodating ground between them. In fine weather, trees that are spaced up to twice the tarp's length will also work. In a storm, the ideal trees would be spaced as close to the tarp as possible, for better support. And of course, choose trees that are sturdy, avoiding any that might topple.

Often, the ground at the base of a tree is somewhat elevated, and this can provide good drainage in the event of rain. The overhead branches can offer several degrees of added warmth at night, by reducing some of the radiant heat loss. And they can help shelter your camp from the nighttime dew.

Wrap each ridge guy around its tree at about stomach height; lower in stormy weather, higher if the trees are farther apart. Then tie the guy back to itself using a taut-line hitch.

Tying a taut-line hitch

Wrap the ridge guy around the tree, then loop it around itself, passing the end through the loop.

Wrap the end through the loop a second time.

The third wrap goes outside the loop, but inside itself.

Tighten the knot securely,

but do not over-tension the guy.

Taut-line hitch

Use the taut-line hitch to attach a ridge guy to a tree, for example. This knot is adjustable, and quite secure when properly tightened. Tighten the knot by grasping it between the thumb and index finger of one hand, and using the same digits of other hand to pull the two lines that extend from the knot, one line at a time. Once the knot is tight, adjust it by sliding it along the line, toward or away from the tarp. Create only enough guy tension to prevent the ridge from sagging excessively under the downward pull of the corner and side guys. Too much ridge tension would stress the tarp unnecessarily.

Staking out the corner guys

In fine weather, stake out the four corner guys only, leaving the side guys unused. When staking out the corner guys, you might think of tying a loop at the end of a guy, inserting a stake through this loop and into the ground. But this would position the stake much too far from the tarp. The guys are extra long for the purpose of tying them around rocks, logs, or brush.

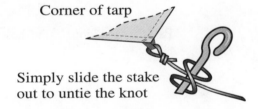

Corner of tarp

Simply slide the stake
out to untie the knot

So instead, tie a clove hitch to the stake a foot or so from the tarp, or closer in stormy weather, then place the stake in the ground.

The clove hitch is adjustable, and it automatically unties itself when you withdraw the stake from the ground and slide the stake out of the knot.

For the best holding power, angle the stake away from the tarp. Optimally, the guy and the stake should form a 90-degree angle.

Tying a clove hitch

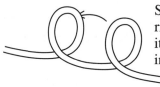

Hold the guy in both hands, thumbs pointing toward each-other, but at a 45 degree angle away from you. Without letting go, make a rabbit-ear loop as shown by twisting the cord in the right hand. Pinch the loop's cross-over point with the left thumb and index finger.

Slide the right hand along the guy to the right. Twist and make a second loop. Pinch its cross-over point with the right thumb and index finger.

Pass the right loop behind the left loop.

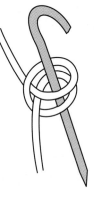

Run the stake through the loops, tighten the line, and press the stake into the ground where you want it.

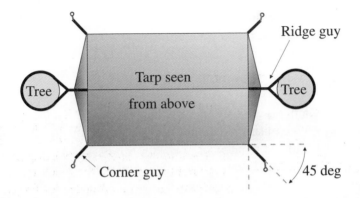

The illustration shows the tarp pitched between two trees, as seen from directly overhead.

In the overhead, or "plan" view, the corner guys should extend away from the corners at an angle of 45 degrees. This angle applies the stress most evenly.

A large wrinkle in the tarp radiating from a corner indicates the need to move the stake to the correct 45-degree angle position.

Securing the side guys

On each side of the ray-way tarp are two side guys. Use these in strong wind to help stabilize the tarp and strengthen it.

Extend the side guys perpendicular to the edge of the tarp, and not too tightly. The best way to determine how tight is to watch the tarp for

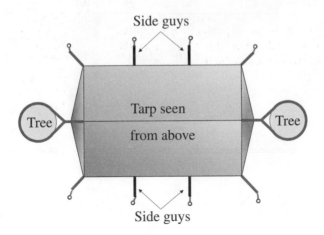

wrinkles. Stiff but not drum-tight, with few wrinkles and no excessive pulling is what we are after. All anchoring options and knots recommended for the corner guys also apply to the side guys. Use stakes if they will hold, or rocks, logs, bushes, downed trees or heavy branches.

Clove hitch quick release

The ray-way tarp kit comes with very thin cord for all but the ridge and corner guys. When using thin cord on a stake, you might find that the clove hitch is difficult to untie, or even slide off. In such a case you could add a quick release to the clove hitch. With a bit of practice, this variation is simple to tie.

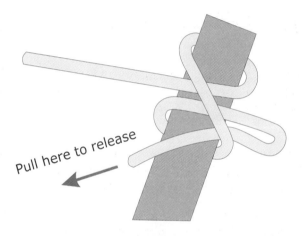

Pull here to release

Incidentally, I sometimes wonder whether the inability to tie these simple tarp knots—the taut-line, sheet bend, clove hitch with and without a quick release, and the overhand on a bight—is one reason many tent campers are reluctant to try a tarp. And yet these knots are very basic and easy to learn. Certainly easier than the knots most of these same people use to tie their shoelaces. If you are unfamiliar with the tarp knots, give them some study, and practice with a length of cord until you can tie each knot skillfully, as you do your shoelaces.

Pitching the tarp between one tree and one support stick

There may be times when you cannot find two suitably spaced trees, but you can find one tree with possible camping adjacent. In such a case you could tie one end of the tarp to the tree, and the other end to a sturdy support stick.

The ideal tarp support stick would be about 4 feet in length and moderately strong. Avoid excessively large support sticks, as they would have more tendency to topple, and could damage the tarp.

Begin pitching the tarp by removing it from its stowbag and locating one of its ridge guys. Tie the guy around the tree at about stomach height, or lower in stormy weather, leaving two or three feet of separation between tarp and tree.

Next, stake out the two corner guys nearest the tree. Simply estimate their position for now. Their only purpose, for the time being, will be to stabilize the tarp as you raise its other end.

Walk around to the other end of the tarp and locate its ridge guy. Secure this guy to the support stick, again at about stomach height or lower in inclement weather. Use a clove hitch, to prevent the line from slipping down the stick. While tying this knot, leave enough space between the tarp body and the stick for the beak. Once you have pitched the tarp and extended its beaks, the ideal separation between beak and stick is about an inch. So while tying the guy to the stick, plan ahead and leave about 16" between stick and tarp body.

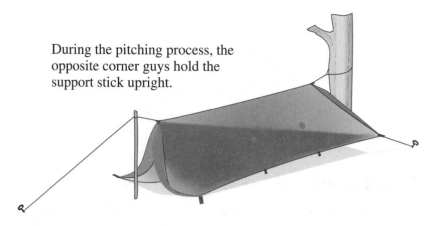

During the pitching process, the opposite corner guys hold the support stick upright.

With the guy tied to the support stick, stand the stick upright. Naturally, it would fall over if you let go. But not if you maintain tension on the ridge guy, pulling in the direction away from the tree. The initial two corner stakes are stabilizing the tarp in a triangular fashion, holding the support stick upright.

So, keeping tension on the ridge guy, stake its end to the ground. Position this stake as far from the tarp as the ridge guy will reach. And angle the stake away from the tarp, such that it's shank is 90 degrees to the guy. This arrangement provides the best holding power.

The tarp is now standing by itself. So, one by one, stake out the two remaining corner guys. Then re-position the initial two stakes with an eye toward creating a taut, wrinkle-free pitch. From there you can tie out the beaks, loosely, one to the tree and the other to the stick, and if desired you can also stake out the side guys and lifters.

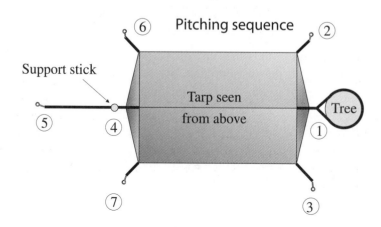

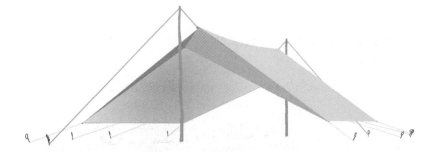

The two support-stick pitching method

The two stick method offers the greatest versatility in site selection, since it does not rely on the availability of trees. Percentage-wise, it is the method Jenny and I use the most.

When pitching the tarp together, one of us holds one support stick upright while tying a ridge guy to it. The other person stakes out the adjacent corner guys, then the ridge guy. That done, we repeat the process at the tarp's other end. And lastly, we re-adjust the corner stakes to create a taut, wrinkle-free and correctly tensioned pitch.

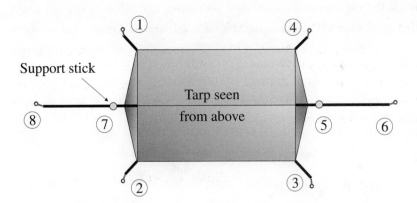

Someone pitching the tarp by him or herself could proceed as follows: Begin by spreading the tarp on the ground and tying its four corner guys to stakes. Then place the stakes into the ground at estimated locations. Tie one ridge guy to a support stick; raise the stick into place, and stake out the guy. The corner stakes are now holding the support stick upright. Repeat the process with the other support stick, then re-adjust the corner stakes for a taut pitch.

Support sticks

To save time searching around camp, Jenny and I normally start looking for tarp support sticks in advance. Where trees and sticks are abundant, a few minutes of hunting will usually suffice. Where they are sparse, we might start looking for them up to an hour before making camp.

If we cannot find sticks that are strong enough, we might use two or more thinner sticks, tying them together at stomach height with the tarp's ridge guy clove hitch, and letting them spread out at the base like a tripod. Where such sticks are not long enough, we have even spiral wrapped a bundle of them with cord, forming a larger stick. This can work surprisingly well.

In desert climes, many times we have used dried stalks of agave or "canes" of saguaro found lying around.

At home we keep a selection of natural tarp support sticks, and sometimes we take a few for use at camp. In the past we have even used hardware-store hardwood dowels, 3/8" diameter.

Aluminum poles or trekking poles would also serve as tarp supports. If they are too slippery to hold the clove hitch, one could wrap the poles in that area with a bit of adhesive tape for a better grip. However my own preference is for natural sticks, as they tend to encourage a better connection with the landscape. Also, they might be safer than metal poles in an electrical storm, in terms of conductivity. At any rate, I find that picking up a couple of sturdy sticks from the ground is no more difficult than pulling aluminum tent poles from the pack and assembling them. In fact, I find it much easier, since I do not have to carry the sticks all day, every day, as I would the poles.

Tarp stakes

In firm ground, the rod type stake with about a seven-inch overall length generally works well. And it occupies less space in the stowbag than the wider, plastic version.

One possible type of stake is that made of hardened (tempered) aluminum alloy, optimally 7075 or 2024-T6 rod, 3/16" diameter. At the top it is usually pre-bent into a hook or nearly into a ring. I normally carry eight of these, in their own stowbag.

Avoid soft aluminum stakes that bend easily. Test by trying to bend the stake slightly by hand. If the stake does not bend without exerting considerable force, then it passes the test. How much force to use? Imagine one hand is the ground and the other is a strong gust of wind striking the tarp and pulling very forcefully on the guy.

Titanium stakes are thinner and lighter than most. They do not tend to hold as well as aluminum in moderate to loose soils because they have less surface area to resist pullout.

Natural anchors: rocks, logs, and bushes

Stakes are convenient but not essential. Natural anchors are present at most sites, and some are much stronger than stakes.

One of the strongest possible tie-points is the base of a nearby bush. While this may seem unlikely, they are often surprisingly well rooted. Wrap a guy around the bush at its base, twice to prevent the line from sliding upwards, then secure the end of the guy back to itself with a taut-line hitch. If concerned about the line cutting into the bush's stem, try wrapping its base with natural materials—dry leaves or grasses or small sticks, making a protective pad.

Another very strong natural tie-point is an exposed tree root. Again, wrap the guy around it twice, then secure with a taut-line hitch. Similar anchoring options might include a nearby tree, or low-lying tree branches.

Another option might be rocks. But a common mistake is to use small rocks—which are usually more available than larger ones—and to pile them on top of each other. Not only does this prevent the person from later adjusting the guy tension, but one tug on the guy, from a gust of wind, will usually bring the pile tumbling down, releasing the guy.

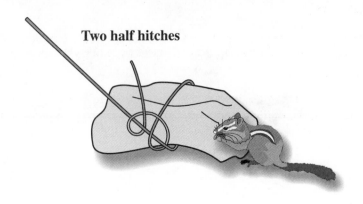

Two half hitches

Instead, use a single, heavy rock per guy; the more flat its bottom, the better. Wrap the guy once or twice around the rock, then secure it with a taut-line hitch or a two half hitches knot. Then give it a test tug. The rock might move surprisingly easily, suggesting the need to find a much larger one, or one with a flatter bottom.

Another tie-point option might be a log, or a heavy tree branch found lying around. Tie the guy to it with a taut-line hitch or two half hitches. Orient the log such that one end points toward the tarp and the other end away from it. This will prevent the log from rolling toward the tarp if pulled by the guy in a heavy gust of wind.

When breaking camp, remember to replace any borrowed rocks, logs, and branches as you found them, same location, same side down. The more aware and in touch with the landscape you become, the more sense this practice will make, for you will begin to notice conspicuous signs such as rocks that an intruder moved and did not replace. Generally, a visitor leaves no evidence, while an intruder—meaning someone with little respect for the landscape—might leave a great deal.

As you practice the various methods of pitching the ray-way tarp, your skills will improve and the process will become easier and more expedient. By selecting natural materials to support and secure the tarp, you will be forging a closer connection with the natural world. And I like to think of trees and sticks, rocks and brush as symbolic of a respite from modern commercialism, a refreshing interlude with nature providing for my needs.

The two-saguaro pitching method

At the Tarp Camp

The ideal wilderness camp would feature a well-pitched tarp, with the knots and stakes or other anchor points checked for security, and the camper's belongings stowed neatly beneath the tarp, including the evening's supply of water for drinking and possibly cooking. Such a camp would be free of belongings left scattered about, and items left outside of reach, such as socks or other articles of clothing hanging from tree branches. This is not so much for neatness as improving a person's chances of not leaving something behind after breaking camp the following morning. And in the unlikely event that the camp needs to be relocated in the middle of the night, because of a bear intrusion or whatever, then an organized camp will be much faster and quicker to strike.

Familiarize and orient

Having establishing a camp such as this, you might find it interesting to wander about the vicinity a short ways, exploring, orienting, and simply absorbing the region's ambience. The more familiar with your "neighborhood," the more comfortable your stay there might be, knowing what is out there. For after all, camping is meant to be much more than simply crawling into a tent and zipping the door shut. So try to glean the most enjoyment from your camp and its environs, by getting in touch with them.

In addition to physically exploring the region, you might sit in quiet observation, perhaps while leaning against the base of a nearby tree. Use all your senses, not only your sight, absorbing the interesting sounds and scents that characterize your little biosphere.

This familiarizing can take as little as a minute, or as long as an hour or more. And if you extend your "connection time" past sundown, you may notice an interesting change in nature's cadence, as the denizens of the day retire and those of the night take their place.

Preening the sleeping area

Having chosen your site with an eye to minimizing impact, as you crawl beneath the tarp you might have to clear the actual area where you will sleep, removing any small sticks, stones, pinecones or their sharp-tipped scale fragments that could puncture your groundsheet. These materials you could disperse, or simply set aside with the intent of spreading them back over the site before you leave. As much as possible, avoid disturbing the area unnecessarily. For example, any excavating of the site is undesirable. And be sure to leave the forest litter, dry leaves and needles in place, as they protect the microcosm beneath the surface, and will also cushion your bed.

The groundsheet

In Beyond Backpacking I discuss the groundsheet and other camping-related items at length. Basically, the groundsheet serves as the tarp's "floor," helping keep your foam pad and bedding free of dirt and sap, and isolating them from any residual ground moisture. The groundsheet may become soiled, but when breaking camp you simply fold it soiled-sides together.

One of the least expensive and most serviceable groundsheet materials is ordinary hardware-store polyethylene, 3-mil thickness. This is the same material used for making poly-tarps.

To reduce its weight and bulk, you could trim the groundsheet to your "sleep-print." Lie on the groundsheet while someone draws a line around you, leaving about twelve extra inches all the way around. Have them leave even more if you would like additional flooring for a few of your belongings. Then with scissors, cut the sheet along the line.

The two-person groundsheet of the type that Jenny and I have used on numerous outings is 81" in length, and 40" wide at the head, 48" wide at the shoulders, and 34" wide at the foot. It is 3-mil polyethylene and weighs about 6 ounces.

A somewhat lighter material is 1.3 oz. silicone-coated nylon, the same used in making tarps. If you will be camping on wet ground, however, choose polyethylene because it is a little more waterproof when laid on.

Thin foam pad

Only when camping on snow, or in a compacted established campsite, would one need a self-inflating mattress, or other type of bulky foam pad.

In most cases a thin foam pad will do. My preference is a closed-cell polyethylene pad about 3/8" thick, of the type usually available in sporting goods and department stores. Before each journey Jenny and I buy a new pad (generally 72" long and 20" wide) and cut it in half, making two shorter pieces. Jenny gets one, and I the other. Then we trim each to shoulder and hip width to eliminate unnecessary weight and bulk. The pads need only match our "torso prints." Specifically, our pads are 36" long, 20" wide at the shoulder and 17" wide at the bottom.

Often, I find even this pad unnecessary, especially when camping on leaves, needles, or duff—nature's version of the foam pad. Even bare, untrammeled dirt is often reasonably soft.

The quilt

When retiring beneath the tarp for the night, and peeling off the hiking or boating clothing, we may check it, and ourselves, for ticks, then set it aside or hang it on the clothesline strung beneath the tarp, end to end. Then we might have a sponge bath, wetting a small hand towel each, and scrubbing one's skin with it. Changing into sleeping clothing (used also on cold days) we crawl comfortably beneath the quilt.

Usually we will have cooked and eaten our evening meal a few hours earlier. But we might snack on a few leftovers, or Jenny might dig out something from the food bag. Either way, we make sure all food items are put away when finished.

The quilt is something I designed as part of our lightweight system, and we have used various quilts on most of our long hikes and paddling adventures. We have found them so effective that we recommend quilts for other campers also, particularly couples. The part of the sleeping bag underneath us adds little to our warmth. As we lie on the insulation, we compress it flat. The quilt dispenses with the part of the sleeping bag under us, and therefore it saves that amount of weight and bulk.

For more information on the quilt, please refer to Beyond Backpacking.

Breaking camp

The morning's routine of breaking camp is essentially a repeat of the previous evening's set-up, in reverse. We change back into our active, day clothing, stow the sleeping garments, stuff the quilt into its stowbag, roll up the foam pads, and pack away other loose items. Often we leave the groundsheet in place, and use its clean, upper surface on which to fold the tarp prior to stowing. But on a rainy morning we stow everything but the tarp while beneath its shelter, then emerge and strike the tarp last.

Folding and stowing the tarp

When taking down the tarp, I find it best to fold and roll it. Trying to stuff or cram it into its stowbag would trap air, making the wad of air-filled nylon much too large for its stowbag.

So while striking the tarp, I first untie its side and corner guys from their anchor points, leaving the tarp hanging from its ridge guys. This folds the tarp naturally in half along its ridge. Untying the ridge guys from their supports, with one hand I then hold the ridge mid-span, and with the other I grasp both ends of the ridge. This folds the tarp in half lengthwise, making the ridge half as long. I fold the tarp in half a second time lengthwise, making the ridge one fourth as long. Then I lay the folded tarp on the groundsheet, if available, and position the guys onto the tarp, being careful not to bunch them together, as this can cause tangles later. Folding the beaks onto the tarp, I create a rectangle. This rectangle I fold in thirds, tucking the guys neatly inside. This produces a long, narrow strip, with the ridge at one end. The strip I then roll tightly, starting from the ridge. This squeezes out most of the air, and allows the tarp to fit easily into its stowbag.

Departure

Once Jenny and I have packed our belongings, and loaded them into the backpacks, canoe or kayak, we check the area very carefully for anything left behind. Then we look at the camp in general, to make sure we are leaving it as we found it. If we had brought in any rocks as guy anchors, we take them back, and put each one where it was, same side down. If we had moved any sticks from the tarp site, we put them back. This simple process is intended to restore the site to its original condition. That way, the next campers here will find the area undisturbed, and will have a chance to enjoy it as much as we did.

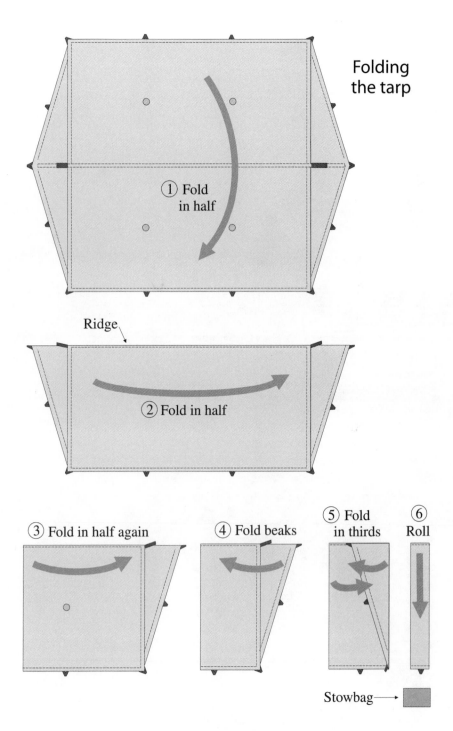

Folding the tarp

① Fold in half

Ridge

② Fold in half

③ Fold in half again

④ Fold beaks

⑤ Fold in thirds

⑥ Roll

Stowbag

The Tarp in Wind

The ray-way tarp is a natural choice in blustery weather, thanks to its all-tension design, its guys securing it to the ground from each of its focal stress areas, and its geometric adaptability, enabling it to be pitched high or low depending on the wind.

In most situations, the silicone-nylon tarp material is more than adequately strong. But if planning to use the tarp in high wind conditions, you might consider making your tarp of urethane-coated nylon, and fitting it with stouter guys. These materials stretch less, enabling the tarp to maintain its shape better in very strong wind.

Site selection

When looking for a campsite on a windy day, consider descending to less windy terrain. Look for a naturally protected glen, or shelter behind natural objects such as boulders, tall brush, or a stand of trees. At the same time, be careful not to pitch the tarp directly against such an object, since the wind could abrade the tarp against it and cause a hole. And too, keep your abode clear of any dead trees or overhead branches that might topple in a gust.

Mode of pitching

Whether the wind is light or strong, try to pitch the tarp sideways to it. In other words, orient the tarp's ridgeline perpendicular to the wind's direction. That way, the tarp will block the wind rather than funnel it.

In strong wind, pitch the tarp lower. This strengthens the pitch and enables the tarp to shed the wind better. Also, the lower the pitch, the more the tarp's beaks angle downward to help block the wind. For even better protection, lower the tarp's windward edge flush to the ground.

To pin the windward edge of the tarp flush to the ground—and only when doing so—insert the stakes directly into the tarp's corner and side pull loops, without using the guys themselves. Or, if not using stakes, secure the guys a few feet from the edge of the tarp—each guy to a rock, log, tree trunk, or the base of a bush—then set a heavy, flat-bottomed rock on each guy, as close to the tarp as possible without actually touching it. Were you to place the rock directly on the fabric, it could chafe or hole it. This tarp is quite strong under tension; its thinness is a concern only should it contact a rough or sharp object, and this is nearly always avoidable.

Ground suitable for stakes

Soft or even moderately consolidated ground might not hold stakes well in strong wind. Once you have placed a stake, and have attached a guyline to it, test by pulling the line in the same direction that the tarp would pull on it. If the stake pulls out, you might have to replace it with a heavy rock, or some other natural anchor. Even if a stake feels only slightly loose, it may not sustain a strong gust.

The ground in most forests is often covered with a layer of leaf or needle litter or duff, and this is usually too soft to hold stakes securely. Sometimes you can dig a small hole in this soft layer, using the heel of your shoe, and expose firm dirt that will hold a stake well. Place a stake into this dirt, attach a guy to it, and give it the pull test. If the stake wobbles, try tamping the earth with the heel of your shoe. Test again, and if successful then dig similar small holes at each of your stake points. Remember to reverse the impact the following morning when breaking camp, by replacing each small pile of duff into its original hole.

Using judgment

Suppose you have pitched the tarp sideways to the wind, and lowered its windward edge flush to the ground. Very well, but what if the storm intensifies during the night, and the wind changes direction? The wind could then blow through the tarp's interior, possibly bringing rain or snow. Rising in the middle of the night, you would have to take the tarp down, and re-pitch it perpendicular to the new wind. That is, assuming the ground slope allows, and that there are no interfering trees, rocks, or bushes close by.

The solution is easier than that. It is called being aware of possibly changing conditions, and preparing for "unforeseen" circumstances.

Before pitching the tarp, consider the wind and sky. If the weather seems likely to deteriorate, think about descending to lower and more protected terrain, and looking for at least some shelter behind natural objects. Either way, pitch the tarp much lower than you would in stable weather, and secure the guys well.

However, you need not pitch the tarp extremely low-lying each and every evening, on the theory that a storm could eventuate. If the weather seems stable, go ahead and trust it. Should an increasing wind catch you by surprise, all is not lost. For you can lower the tarp at any time, by simply lowering the ridge, and re-adjusting the guys.

When pitching the tarp in deteriorating weather, keep in mind that its ridge need not be horizontal, or parallel with the ground. You could pitch the foot end lower than the head, creating a downward sloping ridge. The foot-end beak can touch the ground, if you deem it necessary to block the wind at the foot end. But try to pitch the head end higher for more ventilation. The sloped ridge is acceptable in fine weather also, should you be unable to find a sufficiently long support stick for the foot end.

So plan ahead. Assess the weather, and pitch the tarp accordingly. And remember my tarp adage: The stronger the wind, the lower the pitch. The lower the pitch, the stronger the tarp.

The Tarp in Rain

The ray-way tarp is particularly well suited to wet weather camping, thanks to its spaciousness and ample ventilation. In fact, with the right techniques and a positive attitude, a rainy night spent camping beneath this tarp can be as comfortable as a night of fine weather.

Selecting a site in rainy weather

The most important rainy day consideration is the selection of an appropriate site, discussed in an earlier chapter.

If you pitched your tarp on sloped ground, and rain starts pouring so hard that it courses downhill onto your site, you might have to use a stick to scrape a V-shaped trench in the ground uphill of your tarp. This will channel the groundwater away from you. However, only in extreme need would you need to dig such a trench; I have done it only twice. If you resort to this, be sure to fill the trench and restore the top layer of forest litter before moving on.

If you cannot find a slight rise or a slope, you may decide to camp on level ground. If that ground is porous, it will absorb the rain and prevent flooding of your site. If the ground is impermeable, and rainwater starts running into your enclave, you might try digging a few holes for the water to drain into. But once again the need for this is quite rare; usually you will find raised or sloped ground somewhere.

Wet ground

Suppose that you have found a suitable site that is elevated above its surroundings, but since rain has been pouring from the sky for hours, the ground is soaking wet. Go ahead and pitch the tarp, place your gear under it, and spread your groundsheet, dry side up.

Because you have pitched the tarp over the wet ground, sheltering it from the rain, that ground will begin to dry. Furthermore, your groundsheet will begin to drive the wetness into the earth. The following morning when breaking camp you may be surprised to find the ground beneath you dry.

No groundsheet is puncture-proof, and with use it will often accumulate small holes and tears. But I have not found these to diminish the groundsheet's utility, even when the ground is wet.

Low but not too low

Unless the wind is quite strong, avoid pitching the tarp so low that its interior makes contact with the quilt or sleeping bag. This would restrict the beneficial ventilation, and dampen your bedding with condensation.

Other rainy day considerations

The methods in this book will have you well on your way to dry and comfortable camping. In Beyond Backpacking I discuss a number of additional rain-related topics, unrelated to tarps but applicable to all campers. Because of their importance I will touch on a few here.

Umbrella

For hikers at least, the umbrella can provide excellent shelter while on the move. In most conditions the umbrella is far preferable to even the most expensive waterproof-breathable rain jacket. This is because when used in lieu of a W/B jacket, it eliminates the clamminess and the sweat-soaking of one's clothing. Even in heavy rain, the umbrella allows the hiker to dress for the temperature rather than the rain, often allowing normal hiking clothing to be worn. And because the umbrella keeps the rain off one's face, and from running down the inside of the jacket and shirt, it adds greatly to comfort.

Hikers and other outdoor enthusiasts could use an umbrella as a shelter during mid-day breaks, and in the late afternoons when cooking a hot meal. The umbrella can be useful also while pitching the tarp, and while puttering about, tending to camp chores. It can be deployed at one end of the tarp to help block the wind there. And it can shelter a person nicely the following morning while breaking camp.

Rain wear

Despite the umbrella's usefulness, a rain parka is essential for use when the wind is strong. In normal hiking situations such winds are uncommon, and this means only that the rain parka should be lightweight and compact, stowing neatly away in the backpack. By way of reference, my home-made waterproof-breathable rain parka weighs six ounces.

In addition, rain pants can add to one's comfort while sitting around a drizzly camp, or when ambling at a leisurely pace. Normally they tend to trap too much body heat and moisture for use during vigorous activity. Nevertheless, they are an important emergency item, to be kept in reserve for a storm that might bring heavy rain, gale-force winds, and lower temperatures.

Care of clothing

The more clothing you bring, the more time and effort you will spend in rainy weather trying to keep it all dry. In wet weather, carry only the garments you need. Normally this means one set for the day's exertions, and one set for relaxing and sleeping beneath tarp and quilt. During the day, keep the camp clothing inside a waterproof stuff sack.

All adventure garments must be fast drying, particularly in wet weather. Except for wool-blend socks, this means 100% synthetics. Avoid cottons and cotton blends. Cotton fibers absorb moisture, making them much slower to dry.

Care of sleeping gear

No matter what kind of quilt or sleeping bag you use, keep it dry. The best way to do that is by stowing it in a waterproof stuff sack. For added insurance, consider adding a waterproof liner, such as a plastic trash bag, inside the stuff sack. In extremely wet conditions, use a similar liner inside the backpack, panniers, or boat bag.

The importance of ample hydration

Staying hydrated in rainy weather can be a challenge, simply because you may not feel like drinking water when so much is falling all around you. And the idea of drinking cold water on a cold day might not appeal, when you are trying to stay warm. But in reality, our bodies need as much water intake on a rainy day as a sunny one. In any kind of weather, activities such as hiking, cycling, and paddling can be quite dehydrating. The more dehydrated we become, the less energetic we will feel, and the more deeply chilled. Good hydration brings energy, warmth and vitality.

One day, several years ago, I was hiking in a pouring, storm-driven rain, carrying my sleeping bag in what I thought was a waterproof stowbag, inside my backpack. Descending to lower terrain at day's end, I pitched the tarp, spread my poly groundsheet on the soaking wet ground beneath the tarp, and pulled out my sleeping bag—only to discover that the bag was thoroughly soaked in the foot area, from the knees down. I wrung out the bag as best I could, then crawled into it and commenced shivering for the next twenty minutes. The night was cold, and snow was now falling heavily. But there beneath my tarp I began to warm. I actually slept surprisingly well, even though a few times in the night I had to wake up and bang the snow from the tarp. The next morning found me toasty warm inside a surprisingly dry sleeping bag. My body's warmth, aided by the tarp's superior ventilation, had dried the bag. And when I loaded my pack and struck the tarp, I walked away leaving a decidedly dry spot of ground the size of my groundsheet, on the otherwise snow-covered terrain.

This was after I had relinquished tents in favor of tarps, and it illustrates the warming, drying effect of the tarp, even in storm conditions. But more importantly, it shows how the tarp can be more forgiving of mistakes than a tent. My mistake had been in trusting a stowbag to be waterproof when it was not. But had I been using a tent, the wet sleeping bag would have stayed that way, and my night would have been a cold one.

The Tarp in Other Environments

Snow

The ray-way tarp is a three-season shelter, not intended for winter use. But if adventuring in the higher elevations of the western United States, you could be caught in a surprise snowstorm that begins whitening the landscape, even in mid-summer. This is not a fanciful scenario; it has happened to me at least a dozen times.

The usual recommended course of action is to descend to lower elevations quickly. Up here it is cold and snowing; down there it is warmer and merely raining. Up here you will soon have to camp on snow. Down there you would camp on bare, if wet, ground.

In such a situation, good mobility can aid tremendously, and this calls for lightweight gear.

If you cannot descend, look for an area sheltered naturally from the wind. Even if the snow is falling heavily, take the time to locate the most protected tarp site.

For the quickest and strongest pitch, use the two tree method. Otherwise, remember that the weight of snow accumulating on your tarp will require stronger support sticks.

Before pitching the tarp, scrape away as much snow from your site as possible. If the snow is too deep for that, tromp it down.

Pitch the tarp with its edges close to the ground, its ridge higher, and the roof sloped a little more steeply than usual to help encourage the snowfall to slide off. However, if the snowfall is dry and wispy, which is not likely anytime other than winter, then pitch the tarp low-lying for better shelter from blowing spindrift.

If the surrounding snow is deep, secure the guys to rocks, logs, trees both standing and fallen, or brush.

Summer snowstorms rarely last more than a day or two. But the snow itself can be wet and heavy. Since the roof of the tarp is quite large, it can collect a lot of weight, and this could over-stress the tarp, its guys, and anchor points. Occasionally, then, strike the underside of the roof with an open palm, to knock the snow off. A silicone-nylon tarp is more slippery than one made of urethane-nylon, and snow will slide off it more readily. If the deposition refuses to budge, you may have to emerge and scrape away the snow, especially if the snowfall is massive, and piles up along the tarp's sides.

At any rate, the tarp's open ends can be a welcome advantage on a snowy day, when it comes to making steaming cuppas and hot meals without danger of asphyxiation, as would be the case inside a tent.

Since the summer storms are typically short-lived, you will be able to watch from the dry comfort beneath your tarp as the clouds begin to break up, the shafts of sunlight begin playing over the whitened landscape, and the beautiful, late afternoon light sets the mountains aglow.

Desert

The ray-way tarp is particularly well suited to desert climes. Its roominess and openness offer pleasant relief from the cramped confines of a small tent, and encourage a better comprehension of the wide-open landscape. Pitched taller, the tarp facilitates cross-ventilation, helping cool the interior in hot weather. At night, the tarp protects its occupants and their gear from dew. You might even orient the tarp so that one end faces eastward, to receive the sunshine's warmth the following morning.

Desert rain is infrequent, but is well known for flash flooding that leaves vast areas of standing water. These areas are of course the dished, or lower regions. Watch for them ahead of time and avoid camping there. In particular, avoid the salt, or alkali flats, and other expanses of interior drainage.

In a few regions, certainly not all, the desert floor is too hard for driving stakes. But one can almost always use rocks or brush.

Shoreline and riverbank

For those of us who enjoy kayak and canoe touring, the lighter weight and less bulk of a ray-way tarp can work very well, especially when the route involves many portages. Here again this applies to trips in moderate climates, rather than high-latitude ones. But the same Four Point Plan for pitching the tarp applies: climb high camp low; avoid dished ground; look up; minimize impact.

In addition, shoreline and riverbank camping presents a few unique situations that the boater must be aware of. When searching the shoreline for a suitable camp, make sure it permits access to higher ground. Should a violent storm develop, you may need to move up and away from the water. Never camp at a place hemmed in by cliffs, and think twice before camping on a low-lying island.

If touring an ocean shoreline, situate camp well above high tide line. Whether the tides are diurnal or not, this line is usually just that, a thin line of driftwood bits, small shells, dried eel grass, seaweed and other debris. This line of high tide detritus may be very pronounced or quite faint, but if it seems to be entirely lacking, it is probably somewhere above you and the next high tide could reach much higher than you might expect.

Unless your boat is extremely heavy, carry or drag it to camp where you can keep a close watch on it. This suggests the benefits of situating camp reasonably near the water, but again well out of reach of any storm tossed waves. Many boaters have lost their canoes or kayaks in the night, having left them in the water, or too near it.

Small boat travel offers a whole new world of exploration and connection with the landscape. And the tarp can add much to the experience. The boat can even serve as one of the tarp's anchor points.

Cycling considerations

The tarp is the perfect choice for bicycle touring. It takes up little room in the typically small panniers. And it allows the cyclist to travel lightweight, which is particularly important on hilly terrain.

On a rainy day, the tarp could serve as a shed for working on the bike. I have heard of bike enthusiasts sewing together a smaller, separate tarp under which to store their bike during rainy weather.

Further uses

The tarp could serve as a communal cooking area for a small group. It could function as a rain or sun shelter for activities such as painting and sketching, bird watching, wildlife viewing, Vision Questing, botany or other natural history study, as well as for working on aboriginal skills such as flint knapping, basket weaving, carving, and so forth. Due largely to the tarp's lack of floor, and its adjustable height, its applications are virtually unlimited.

Animals and Insects

To someone accustomed to tent camping, the tarp's openness might instill a feeling of vulnerability. Yet such fears are unfounded. The unrestricted flow of sights and sounds beneath a tarp actually adds to security by enhancing one's awareness of the outside world.

Omni ignotum pro magnifico: Everything unknown is taken as grand. In other words, fear of the unknown. And from inside a tent, nearly everything out there is unknown. What is that noise outside? A bear? Were you sleeping beneath an open tarp, you could see that it is only a couple of deer ambling past.

When it comes to wildlife encounters at camp, keep in mind that what the creatures could do to you is not necessarily what they intend to do. Those deer ambling quietly past could suddenly turn and attack you, kicking, stomping and biting. But the chances of them actually doing that are very slim. The same holds true with the other denizens of the wilderness: the bear, cougar, porcupine, field mice, snakes, spiders and ants. Mosquitos and ticks are a different matter, of course, and these I will discuss shortly. But simply because the tarp is open at both ends does not automatically subject its occupants to unpleasant encounters with wild animals.

So the best way to overcome feelings of vulnerability is not to crawl inside a tent, zip the door shut, and hope for the best, like the proverbial ostrich with its head in the sand. Rather, it is to camp in an open shelter that allows you to remain aware of what is happening all around you, while realizing that the creatures roving about during the night are not out to attack you. Most of us enjoy seeing wildlife, and what a pleasant opportunity as we relax quietly beneath our tarps.

At the same time, a few precautions are in order, and these apply to both tent and tarp campers.

Black bears

In black bear country, a close encounter is more likely for someone in a tent than beneath a tarp. The tent camper will usually discover the bear only by its heavy grunting and shuffling just outside the tent wall. And to the bear, that wall is no barrier. Conversely, the person beneath an open tarp may identify the bear at some distance. This can add to safety in two important ways. If the animal knows you have seen it, it will be less inclined to venture near. And if it stubbornly remains in the area, you can pack up and move off.

Also, the tent camper who awakens in the night to discover a bear at the door is essentially trapped. Not so beneath a tarp, which is open at both ends.

But remember that the black bear is after your food, not you. Bears are extremely smell sensitive, and their greatest attractant is the odor of food. Cold food will attract them for perhaps a hundred yards or more, depending on topography and wind. Food that is being cooked will attract them for miles. The odor of cooking food is a long-distance signal odor. And it lingers at campsites for days.

The best way to avoid a bear encounter, then, is not to attract one. And that means cooking miles away from where you camp, usually by pausing for an early dinner, then continuing several more miles before stopping for the evening. It also means camping miles from any established campsites and their attendant signal odors.

But how does one avoid the established campsites in the National Parks, where camping is restricted to the designated areas? By avoiding the National Parks. Instead of visiting Glacier National Park, for example, consider a trip through the regions immediately to the south: the beautiful Bob Marshall and Scapegoat Wilderness areas. Instead of Yellowstone, try the wild Absaroka Range to the east, or the Wind Rivers to the southeast. Give the Yosemite high country a miss in favor of Oregon's Three Sister Wilderness, as Jenny and I once did while filming a BBC documentary.

Rodents

Here again my advice is to avoid established campgrounds, because at these places the field mice and their rodent cousins are usually human habituated. This means they associate campers with their food, and have no compunction about gnawing through food bags to get it. They also gnaw through tents, and this suggests yet another advantage of tarps.

Rodents at the established sites are not being pests; they are only responding to the temptation of food placed at their disposal. And since they are human habituated, they are not afraid to go after it.

Away from established campsites, these creatures rarely associate campers with their food. Squirrels, chipmunks and voles may be your neighbors, but usually they will try to avoid detection. Rarely will they venture close enough to investigate your food bags.

Snakes

Like most other creatures, snakes forage for food. They are looking for mice, insects, and small birds. Not humans. So do not worry about a snake attack while sleeping beneath an open tarp.

Also, a snake would no sooner slither over and bite you than a deer would mosey over and kick you. You are much bigger than the snake, so it is naturally fearful of you. However, if you cornered the deer it might kick, and if you provoked a snake it might try to bite. Any creature will try to defend itself in some way.

Statistically, most snakebites are the result of someone molesting the snake. Or someone doing something that the snake interprets as threatening.

So when selecting a campsite, check for snakes, and avoid camping near a pile of rocks, brush or leaves, which could be snake haunts. If the bushes are thick around your prospective site, probe them with a long stick before pitching your tarp.

In the extremely unlikely event that a snake does come around your camp, move slowly and carefully away from it, and give it time to depart.

Scorpions

Scorpions forage at night for small insects. They are quite timid and afraid of any creature larger than themselves. So there is virtually no danger of one attacking you beneath your tarp at night. However at dawn they do retire into whatever shelter seems best, and this could be a shoe or an item of clothing left lying about. When in scorpion country, check these items carefully before putting them back on.

Ticks

Ticks are parasites that feed on the blood of animals. But ticks do not hunt for those animals. Rather, they cling to brush or grass in hopes that an animal will happen along. If one does, the tick grabs on. So as you lie beneath your tarp, do not worry about armies of ticks roving about in search of prey. If a tick moves three yards, that is a long trip.

One of the tick's favorite hosts is the deer. And deer are creatures of habit. They have their afternoon lays, and their night lays. These lays are often located in concealing brush, and they are evident by the matted appearance of the grass, leaves or pine needles. And they are often teeming with ticks. So when searching for a suitable place to pitch your tarp, avoid camping on a deer lay.

If, during the night, you find what feels like a mole on your skin that you were not aware of, it could be a tick. Do not blame the open tarp; in every likelihood you acquired the tick elsewhere and brought it to your camp unnoticed. And do not pick the tick off you. Rather, sit up, shine a flashlight on it, and use a pair of tweezers to gently but firmly pull the head of the tick from its grasp. As long as you do not squeeze the body, and so inject its toxins into yourself like a hypodermic needle, in all probability the tick will not transmit a disease.

The chances of finding a tick on yourself are about the same whether you sleep in a tent or under a tarp. But the ticks that go undiscovered are the more dangerous, because they can transmit disease as they regurgitate at the natural conclusion of their feeding. Therefore, when in tick habitat check your clothing, body and gear frequently.

Blackflies and mosquitos

Unless they are swarming, blackflies will rarely remain beneath a covered shelter, even one that is open at both ends. They tend to fly in, panic, and fly straight back out. Also, they are inactive at night. So the tarp offers considerable protection from blackflies. As does protective netting and clothing, since blackflies cannot bite through fabric.

Mosquitos will often land on the tarp, on its upper or lower surfaces, and sometimes will remain there for hours, or even throughout the night. So although the open tarp will not protect a person from mosquitos, it will at least reduce their numbers to a small degree.

In *Beyond Backpacking* I describe my system of bug-proof "shell" garments. Used with a head net, these lightweight shells are completely effective against blackflies and mosquitos. You can wear them during the day, and sleep in them at night. Thus, they enable the use of the tarp in just about any degree of bug presence.

In addition, you could sew a length of no-see-um netting to your quilt or bag, and use this to cover your head at night.

The combination of the tarp, the shell garments and head net, and netting sewn to the quilt or bag works extremely well. This is a lightweight and compact setup, and in most situations is my recommended method. It works for flying and biting insects, as well as merely bothersome crawling ones such as ants. For additional protection at camp, you could use a net-tent, as described in the following chapter.

For further discussion on avoiding unpleasant encounters with creatures, see Beyond Backpacking.

Prototype net-tent on the PCT in 1994

The Net-Tent

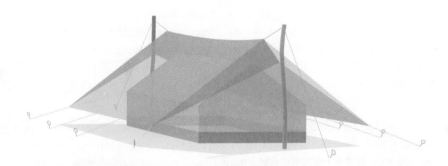

History of the design

Some thirty years ago I sewed a width of bug-proof netting to the perimeter of my nylon tarp. The netting hung from the tarp all around, and the idea, obviously, was to block the insects. But in actual practice it did not work.

To begin, the netting did not rid my tarp enclosure of bugs. As I lay there trying to rest, one by one the mosquitos would rise from the ground and begin pestering me. It seems they had been in the grass and forest litter unnoticed, and when I pitched the enclosure over them, it caged them. And when I swatted at them, the netting prevented their escape. So they were soon back for another attempt at a meal.

Another disadvantage was that since the netting was sewn to the tarp, I could not leave the netting at home when the bugs were few and tolerable, which was most of the time. This meant that I could not rid my backpack of its extra weight and bulk when desired. And even in perfectly fine weather I had to endure the closed-in feeling.

Also, I could not pitch the tarp higher in fine weather, with its edges higher above the ground, since this would have created an open gap below the netting all around. When I pitched the tarp very low in strong wind, the netting got in my way. And when I pitched the tarp low in rainy weather, the netting became soaked and muddy, creating an unsightly mess.

This was one of those experiments that did not work as I had hoped.

But it did teach me that the netting must adjust in height with the tarp as the weather dictates; it has to be removable; and it requires a floor.

Simplicity is often the best solution, however, so after I removed the netting, I slept comfortably beneath the open tarp in shell clothing and a netting face cover, when necessary. This method worked so well that I continue using it to this day.

However, when the bugs are positively swarming, a netting enclosure can be a welcome addition. So as Jenny and I were hiking the PCT southbound with a tarp in 1994, I began to ponder again some kind of an enclosure that would not sacrifice the benefits of the tarp, but that would merely attach to its underside when needed. And it was here that I finally devised a workable plan. I called it the "net-tent."

The idea seemed to have great potential, and we were eager to try it. So while taking a few days off from the journey to attend to business, we sewed together a net-tent. Returning to the trail, we used this bug-free enclosure a short ways along the PCT through central Oregon, at the height of mosquito season. This was only a test, and in the interests of minimizing packweight we soon sent it home. But the tests were so successful that I decided to describe it in my books.

If you would like to try a net-tent, my sincere wish is that you make your own, rather than buy one commercially. For one thing, I know of no commercial net-tents made to my specifications. So I cannot guarantee that your tests with them will prove satisfactory. But cutting out the materials and sewing them together yourself is such a simple and straightforward process, that I am including step-by-step instructions in this book. Also, at the time of this writing I am selling net-tent materials kits. Please see my web site at www.rayjardine.com for details.

Design features of the net-tent

The net-tent is a tent-like enclosure with vertical walls and a sloped, gabled roof made of netting, and a waterproof floor. It has no poles, but simply attaches, when needed, to the underside of the ray-way tarp. Thus, the net-tent gives you protection from mosquitos and other biting insects, while still allowing you to enjoy all the advantages of the tarp. And it is removable, meaning that you can leave it at home when the insects are not likely to be swarming.

The two-person net-tent, made from a ray-way kit, including lines, hooks and cord locks weighs 11.9 ounces.

Specifically, the walls and roof are made of "no-see-um" netting. This has a tighter weave to thwart the tiny bugs that mosquito netting would admit. It is slightly less ventilating than mosquito netting, but not noticeably so. And it weighs about the same.

The floor is waterproof nylon, with a raised rim to help keep the interior clean and dry. The floor serves also as a groundsheet on all but the wettest terrain, saving the weight of a separate groundsheet. However, if the ground is particularly wet, or sooty or grimy as in some campgrounds, or sap-laden as beneath some conifers, then a separate groundsheet might be of use.

The net-tent requires no tent poles or additional support sticks. Rather, it merely clips beneath the tarp with thin suspension lines terminated by small hooks. From these hooks the net-tent hangs under the tarp like a hammock.

The net-tent has a fixed shape, like a tent, but its suspension lines adjust in length. This enables the enclosure to retain its shape despite the tarp's varying geometry.

Entry and exit is via a doorway flap. This arrangement eliminates the zipper. This is important because zippers are notoriously vulnerable. Imagine pitching your tent and crawling inside to escape the hungry hoard, only to discover that the doorway zipper no longer works. This is not a fanciful scenario, for it has sent innumerable campers home, ahead of schedule. It will not send you and your net-tent home. And of course the absence of zippers eliminates their weight and bulk.

Set up

To begin setting up the net-tent, first pitch the tarp using one of the methods explained earlier in this book. Try to avoid pitching the tarp excessively high or low, as this would limit the use of the net-tent. In fine weather, pitch the tarp about waist-high. This allows the tarp's roof angle, or slope, to more closely match that of the net-tent.

Remove the net-tent from its stowbag, and spread it beneath the tarp, floor-side-down. Make sure that the netting is on the floor rather than the ground, to keep the netting clean. Decide which end of the tarp you want the netting doorway to face. Ordinarily you would sleep inside the enclosure with your head toward its doorway. Then orient the net-tent so that its ridgeline lies more or less parallel to that of the tarp.

Each of the net-tent's suspension lines enters the netting through a tiny, reinforced hole, and is fitted with a cord lock located inside the enclosure. These cord locks enable you to adjust the net-tent to the particular tarp pitch.

Before you suspend the net-tent, check that these cord locks are pulled all the way out to their keeper knots. This will facilitate the set up, at least your first few times. Once you have more experience, you might choose to leave the ridge suspension lines at about the correct length.

Suspension

To suspend the net-tent beneath the tarp, proceed as follows:

1) Ridge: Start at the head of the net-tent, and clip the ridge hook to the tarp's clothesline loop. Move around to the foot, and clip its ridge hook into its clothesline loop.

2) Corners: Hook the four net-tent corner lines, one at a time, to their adjacent tarp corner guys, where the guys attach to their pull loops.

Note that the tarp has no special loops to accept these hooks. Rather, the hooks simply wrap around the tarp's corner guys, where those lines meet the tarp's pull loops.

3) Shoulders: Attach the net-tent's shoulder lines, one on each side, to the tarp's adjacent side guys. These expand the net-tent's interior laterally at the shoulder area.

Entry

To enter the net-tent, lift its doorway flap and crawl through the opening. The netting material is relatively delicate, so be careful not to snag it while making haste to escape the mosquitos or blackflies. If the bugs are numerous and aggressive, you will likely be wearing bug-proof clothing. This clothing would eliminate the need to rush madly into your shelter.

Once inside, draw each suspension line through its cord lock to give the net-tent its proper shape. There is no need to over-tighten, as this would tend to lift the net-tent were it empty, and distort and stress it unnecessarily when occupied.

Keeping bugs out

Once inside with your sleeping gear and any other items needed during the night, spread the doorway flap on the floor, such that it extends into the shelter about 10 inches. Then weigh the flap down with anything handy—a couple of water bottles, or items of spare clothing for example.

If mosquitos or blackflies have followed you in, you could lift the doorway flap and herd them back out, as I usually do, or you could exterminate them. The reason I normally chase them out is one of sanitation. Smashing too many onto the netting can eventually make it smell like rotting fish. The fetid odor is difficult to remove, even with repeated launderings.

In my experience, the flap-type door thwarts all types of flying insects, and the vast majority of crawling ones. Still, an occasional ant could find its way into the enclosure. This would be a minor nuisance in most cases, rather than a real threat. Unless, perhaps, it is a fire ant of the Southwest, in which case you would be careful to avoid their haunts to begin with.

Any type of ant that breaches a net-tent is typically searching for food. Ants are scavengers and opportunists, but are also drawn by odors of food or something that might be food. The ant is not trying to attack you; it is merely after your cookie crumbs, or other types of food or scraps. By keeping your enclosure clean, the ants will most likely stay out.

Ticks can be a concern, because unlike ants they crave your blood. Whether using a tent or tarp and net-tent, avoid camping on a deer lay, as these can harbor ticks galore. Normally, however, ticks are few, and they tend to be dormant at night. If you awaken to find one on you, you probably carried it into your shelter yourself.

Used as a groundsheet and netting cover

Wind and rain usually deter mosquitos and blackflies, eliminating the need for the net-tent. This allows you to pitch the tarp low-lying for optimal protection from the elements.

However, you could spread the net-tent on the ground beneath the low-lying tarp, and without connecting the netting to the tarp, simply crawl into it like a sleeping bag. The netting would add a bit of warmth. And should the wind subside during the night and the bugs return with a vengeance, the netting would add to your protection.

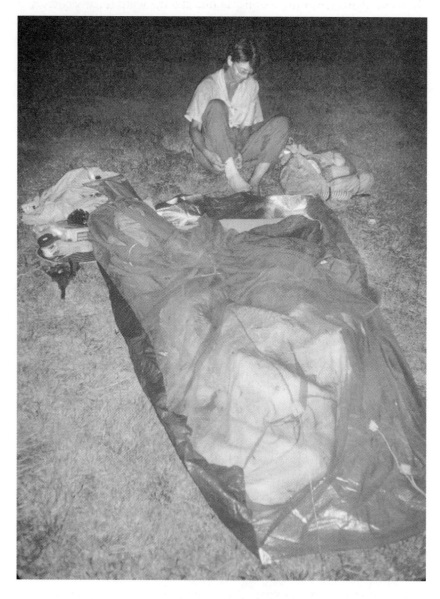

Using the net-tent as a groundsheet and cover.

On the PCT in 1994

Used as a stand-alone shelter

On those nights when the weather is fine and the wind relatively calm, a tarp might not be necessary, at least in the absence of dew. But if the insects are swarming and discouraging you from sleeping under the stars, you might consider pitching the net-tent as a stand-alone shelter. The idea is to pitch it as though it were a tarp, using much the same methods. If you are using two support sticks, they should be about the same length. You may need to extend the lines so they will reach your chosen trees or support sticks, and your stakes or anchor points. In other words, you may have to tie additional cords to the existing net-tent lines. Be sure to tension the lines only lightly to avoid deforming and possibly damaging the netting.

Stowing the net-tent

When breaking camp, the temptation might be to leave the net-tent attached to the tarp, striking both together and stowing as a single unit. More often than not, though, this would lead to a tangle of lines and fabric that would complicate the next evening's set-up rather than simplify it.

So, before emerging from the shelter, slacken its lines. Then once outside, unhook the lines from the tarp. This will make for an easier pitch the following evening.

If you wad the net-tent and cram it into a stuff-sack, it will occupy more space in your backpack than necessary. A better method is to fold and stow. Here is how:

After you have unclipped the net-tent from the overhead tarp, stretch out its floor to its original size and shape. Lay the netting and cords onto its floor, then fold the floor in half. This clam-shells the netting and lines inside the folded floor. Fold again, then lay out the net-tent's stowbag nearby to help you judge the final folds, to arrive at the correct sized package.

Tarp and net-tent combo

Used together, the tarp and net-tent offer a cozy shelter-like feel, and protection from rain and bugs. But because of their versatility, the tarp and net-tent offer many advantages over conventional tents. One is the improved ventilation that will help keep you drier and warmer. Another is the option of pitching the shelter higher in mild weather, for added ventilation and peripheral views, or pitching it lower in stormy conditions for reduced wind resistance. And too, when the bugs are few, you can leave the net-tent home to reduce your packweight and bulk.

For less than a pound you get a bug shelter that does not rely on fragile tent poles or zippers, and that takes up very little space in your backpack or gear bag.

The net-tent is simple in design and straightforward in construction. Sewing one yourself is not difficult, and can save you money over buying one commercially. For details, refer to the sewing instructions later in this book.

Options not Advised

Tarps with curved hoops

Tarps with hoops or curved poles are made more for aesthetics and convenience of use, than robustness. This suggests their designers had not used their creations in stormy conditions. In general, these shelters are poorly resistant to high wind, and poorly anchored, meaning they can be blown away. When it comes to poorly designed camping shelters, "Gone With the Wind" is not just the name of a classic movie.

Single-walled tent

The single-walled tent is of course lighter than an equivalent contemporary tent with rainfly. Some small single-walled tents made of lightweight materials weigh very little. Still, they represent a step backward in the evolution of camping shelters. Like going from a round wheel to a beautiful square one. Why? Because they do not ventilate. At least conventional tents with the separate rainfly attempt to remedy the paucity of ventilation. Single-walled tents simply ignore it. Even ones made of waterproof/breathable material, which in terms of breathability is closer to vapor barrier material than to uncoated nylon. And large vents are of little help.

Klondike: *I just returned from a backpacking trip with my brother in the Smokies. We used his new "light weight" single wall tent. This tent, from a major manufacturer, had 1' x 4' vents with awnings along the bottom of both sides, one 1' x 1' vent at the top and one small vent in the vestibule. We had excessive condensation inside the tent. It was so bad, that one night, the impact of the raindrops sprayed the condensation on us. The next trip we are going to use my home-made tarp.*

Tarp-tent

Some types of single-walled tents are pitched between trees or external support sticks, based, obviously, on the ray-way tarp that preceded them.

These so-called tarp-tents are poorly ventilating, especially with their doorways closed. Open doorways admit rain and wind. Thus, these types share the disadvantages of single-walled commercial tents, mentioned above, with a few added disadvantages of their own. They have no floor in many cases, so they cage mosquitos and other on-site insects. And they are poorly resistant to strong wind, even when pitched lower.

Bivy sack

The bivy sack might seem like a viable option, since it is lighter and more compact than a tent. Some types are complex in design; some are equipped with hoops or poles and resemble miniature tents. All types tend to be extremely restrictive of the all-important ventilation. Which is why they are often referred to as "sweat sacks." Most are heavier than a ray-way tarp, for a mere fraction of the living space. Meaning they provide no place to shelter one's backpack or other belongings, no place to hang wet clothing, and certainly no place to cook out of the rain.

Hammocks

I have gained considerable experience with hammocks, both at camp and on the high cliffs of Yosemite and elsewhere, so am familiar with their advantages and disadvantages. Here is my estimation of how this "shelter" compares with the ray-way tarp.

Commercial, overnight hammocks typically come with waterproof awnings, protecting their occupants from rain. However, models that feature secure, well-stabilized awnings tend to be heavy. And lightweight hammock awnings are easily displaced by strong wind, leaving the occupant fully exposed to the rain. Be careful of marketing hype. Before you set off into the wilderness with this type of shelter, know its limitations.

Even the lightest and smallest covered hammocks weigh about 1½ pounds. This means that a one-person hammock is a half-pound heavier than a two-person ray-way tarp.

The hammock requires two trees or other very stout supports. The manufactures suggest that where trees are sparse or absent, one is to sleep on the ground, covered with the hammock and its awning. I do not know many people who could camp comfortably this way, particularly in stormy weather.

The hammock suspends over vegetation, rather than crushing it, and where the vegetation is pervasive this can reduce the camper's impact. Sounds good, perhaps, for those headed for the jungles. Yet even in dense tropical rainforests, or the lush woodlands of the continental US, the vegetation is rarely so pervasive that a camper could not locate a minimum-impact tarp site.

In theory, the hammock allows one to camp on a steep timbered slope. But what about the person's gear? Drop a sleeping bag in its cylindrical stowbag, for example, and it might tumble all the way to the base of the slope—where, by the way, one could camp with greater ease and security using a tarp.

Anything from three to six feet above the ground is in the zone of maximum visibility. This means that a person in a hammock is visible in most cases from quite a distance. While some campers prefer to advertise their presence in the woods, others might feel safer maintaining a low profile.

The hammock forces a person to lie on his or her back or side, which is fine. But it also forces the body into a banana shape. This might be comfortable for some people, especially those who enjoy sleeping on waterbeds and slouching in overstuffed chairs at home. But it bends and twists the spine, and tends to stretch the ligaments connecting and stabilizing the vertebrae. The more stretched these ligaments become, the weaker the person's back and the more prone to injury and other maladies. For the strongest back, sleep on a firm, reasonably flat surface.

When not to use a Tarp

Lack of knowledge

The ray-way tarp has the potential for sheltering its occupants safely and comfortably in stormy weather. But only the potential. If pitched incorrectly, or used incorrectly, it may not work as expected.

The same holds true for a tent. In a sudden, unexpected storm, the tent must go up quickly. But if the person is unfamiliar with its pitching methods, he or she might struggle and expend precious body warmth, only to have the tent collapse in a gust. This would not be the shelter's fault, but the inexperienced person who neglected to practice with it in advance.

If you are new to tarp camping, take heart. You can easily learn the methods by reading this book. And you can familiarize yourself with the tarp's set-up, by practicing in your backyard, at a nearby park, or at some other convenient location.

Once familiar with the pitching methods, if some uncertainty remains, you might take both tent and tarp on a few overnight outings. Pitch the tarp, and leave the tent stowed in its bag as a backup. If you have studied this book and practiced near home, your tarp will very likely perform flawlessly. If something does compel you to revert to the tent, figure out why, and make the necessary corrections next time.

Generally there are only three things that could go wrong with the tarp set-up.

• One, rainwater flows toward the tarp and invades your living quarters. Here again, this is caused by selecting dished ground for a campsite. The solution is to camp on slightly elevated, or sloped ground.

• Two, the wind blows through the tarp's interior. Again, pitch the tarp sideways to the wind, if necessary pin the upwind edge of the tarp to the ground. And in very strong wind, pitch the tarp very low-lying.

• The third problem is human error: knots tied incorrectly, a poor choice of support sticks, guys that are not well anchored, and so forth.

Each of these errors is easily avoided by following the instructions in this book.

Harsh environments

The tarp is of course not suitable for use in wintry conditions, including heavy snowfall and deeply snowpacked terrain. Many other environments are too harsh for the tarp, mainly those renowned for gale-force winds, very low temperatures, heavy rain, sleet and snow, and unaccommodating terrain. Places such as northern Canada and Alaska, parts of Iceland, the United Kingdom, and of course the Himalayas, Tierra del Fuego, etc. The extreme conditions of these locales calls for something more substantial than a lightweight, three-season shelter, be it a tarp or a tent.

Starry nights

For the kind of camping that most of us enjoy, there may be nights so mild that no type of shelter is needed. Nights where the air is still, the sky cloudless, and the dew is negligible. Nights such as these can be savored under the glorious sweep of stars.

Making and Using a Poly-Tarp

The poly-tarp is a no-frills yet very serviceable shelter, easily made from ordinary hardware-store plastic sheeting. This material is called polyethylene, and it requires no sewing or other assembly.

At the time of this writing, my local hardware store sells a roll of 3-mil clear poly, 10 feet wide by 25 feet long, for $4.29. This would make a pair of 2-person tarps, each measuring 10 feet by 9.5 feet, at a cost of only $2.15 per tarp. The leftover plastic could be used for groundsheets. For someone on a budget, this is low-cost camping at its best.

Because of its low cost and ease of use, the poly-tarp can provide a very practical introduction to tarp camping. Making one can be fun and rewarding, and a good way to interest children in camping. Youngsters love sleeping under these see-through plastic shelters. And so do we adults.

Which is not to suggest that poly-tarps are mere playthings. I have camped under them an estimated 300 nights in the Colorado Rockies, in all sorts of weather.

Recommended material: 3-mil polyethylene

Clear, plastic polyethylene is waterproof, and widely available at hardware stores and building supply centers. 3-mil is my recommended thickness, for it is adequately storm-proof when well cared for, yet reasonably lightweight.

Weight of polyethylene

3-mil polyethylene weighs about 2 ounces per square yard.

So for example, a two-person poly-tarp measuring 10' x 9.5' would weigh about 21 ounces. That is a very spacious shelter for a mere 1 pound 5 ounces, or about a third the weight of even the lightest two-person tents and their rainflys.

A one-person poly-tarp, measuring a palatial 10' x 7' weighs about 15 ounces.

By way of comparison, silicone-coated nylon weighs about 1.3 ounces per square yard. This is 65% of the weight of 3-mil poly.

Materials not recommended

A few materials not recommended would include polyethylene that is thinner than 3 mil, which is not strong enough, and polyethylene that is thicker than 3 mil, which is too heavy.

Tyvek is used mainly in the building industry as "house wrap," and is usually available at hardware and building supply stores. It weighs about 1.3 ounces per square yard, but is not waterproof and therefore unsuitable for use as camping tarps and other gear. One could treat it with a waterproofing compound, but this would add weight and noxious odors, and may have a limited service life.

Reflective silver mylar, sometimes known as Space™ blanket material, is waterproof, and at a mere 0.56 ounces per square yard is extremely lightweight. But it is so thin and tears so easily that it cannot survive much wind. For this reason I do not recommend it as a tarp material, even in moderate climates.

Size of poly-tarp

The poly-tarp should be long enough to shelter its occupants from any wind-driven rain, and it should be wide enough to offer protection from the splatter of rebounding rain, which can occur along the sides.

As a general guideline, I suggest you cut the polyethylene so that, when pitched, the poly-tarp affords a 2-foot margin between its occupants and the edges of the tarp on all sides.

Note that such a wide margin does not ordinarily apply to a sewn ray-way tarp, because of its side guys, lifters and beaks.

So, for example, if making a one-person poly-tarp, you would add 4 feet to your height. That would be my suggested length. For the width, suppose your bedding is 2 feet wide; then the roof should cover a width of 6 feet. But the tarp material must be wider than that, due to the slope of the roof. The optimum roof angle, when pitching the tarp in fair weather, is 34 degrees. So the material width would be 6 / cos 34° = 7.2 feet.

• For one person, the poly-tarp would be 10 feet long and 7 feet wide.

• For two people: 10 feet long and 9.5 feet wide.

• For three people: 10 feet long and 12 feet wide.

• And for four people: 10 feet long and 14 feet wide.

Note that beneath a three-person tarp, the occupants could lie parallel to the ridge, or perpendicular to it. Beneath a four-person tarp, lying perpendicular to the ridge gives more room.

To accommodate more than four people, one would make additional poly-tarps as necessary.

Ben B.*: I am making a poly-tarp for two people, but it seems big to me. I may just not be used to the large, light size.*

For campers accustomed to the cramped confines of a small backpacking tent, the poly-tarp can seem huge. And indeed, in fine weather the large amount of sheltered area might be considered excessive. But in a storm we need the generous roof size, keeping in mind that rain does not always fall straight down, nor does it splash straight up.

Karl K.*: Does the poly-tarp benefit from lifters and beaks like on your nylon tarp designs? I know the point of the poly-tarp is to keep it simple, but I have added beaks as part of the project.*

Someone who does not sew might be tempted to add the ray-way tarp's features to the poly-tarp, using duct tape and so forth. And how true that one of the great advantages of inexpensive polyethylene is its ease of experimentation. You can use it to test all sorts of ideas.

However, one of its limitations is its vulnerability to tearing at any cuts, notches or sharp-angled concavities. So for example you might be tempted to cut a notch from each end and duct-tape the edges together to form beaks. But in so doing you would create a very large stress riser at each end. This would weaken the tarp enormously.

I recommend keeping the shape a simple rectangle, as this is quite strong. If you want the greater coverage and protection similar to what the ray-way beaks provide, simply size your rectangular poly-tarp larger. This of course would add weight, and if you are interested in reducing the tarp's weight, then you might consider the many advantages of sewing a nylon tarp.

Poly-tarp lines

The poly-tarp uses one continuous line, strung from tree to tree, to support the tarp's ridge. In most cases, 30 feet of line would serve amply as a ridge line.

Use stout line, at least 4mm in diameter. Most types would function well. My choice is braided Dacron: braided for its superior handling, and Dacron for its strength, longevity, and resistance to UV-b degradation. Nylon line would also work well. Polypropylene line handles and holds knots poorly.

In addition to the ridge line, the poly-tarp requires four corner guys. These can be 1/8" diameter, and about 5 feet long each.

The corner guys attach to the tarp with sheet bend knots, as described in the chapter near the beginning of this book. Tie these knots before using the tarp for the first time, and leave them for the life of the tarp. The sheet bends are extremely strong. Properly tied, I have not seen one pull out.

Ben B.*: I was planning on using military 550 cord for the ridgeline and also the corner ties. Would it be wise to pull the core out of the cord to save weight or should I leave it in for strength and also in case I need small sewing line, dental floss, or the like?*

The military 550 type cord would be fine for the ridge line, as is. For the corner guys you could extract the core and use only the sheath. Due to raveling, the core is unsuitable as guys.

Tim M.*: I am using a tarp for my AT thru-hike, and I read your advice on using a sheet bend knot on the poly-tarp's corners rather than grommets. Is there any knot that can be effectively used along the tarp edge?*

Sheet bend knots at the corners are so strong that the poly-tarp does not require side guys. In stormy weather you would pitch the tarp's sides close to the ground. And in very strong wind you could even use rocks to pin the edges down. Use smooth rocks, to avoid tearing the plastic material.

Methods of pitching the poly-tarp

The methods of pitching the poly-tarp are similar to those of pitching the ray-way tarp. Refer to that information, with the following exceptions for the poly-tarp:

Unlike the ray-way tarp, the poly-tarp is supported by a continuous ridge line. When pitching the poly-tarp between two trees, use a taut-line hitch at both ends. Adjust one of the hitches to stretch the line very tightly. Next, drape the tarp over the line, with half of the poly material hanging down one side, and half the other. Finally, stake out the four corner guys.

To pitch the poly-tarp between one tree and one support stick, tie the ridge line to the tree first, then spread your poly-tarp over the line and temporarily stake out the two corner guys nearest the trees. Walk to the other end of the tarp and tie the ridge line to the support stick, using a clove hitch to prevent the line from slipping down. Raise the tarp by its ridge line, tie the line's end to a stake as usual, and tension the line tightly. Then stake out the other two corner guys, and adjust the initial two guys to achieve a proper pitch.

The procedure for using two support sticks is much the same. Of course, it helps to have another person to lend a hand, but it is entirely possible to pitch the tarp yourself. Here is how: Extend your ridge line across the ground where you want your tarp to be. Lay the poly-tarp over the line, as though pitching it. Stake out the corner guys in approximately the right locations. Now proceed to erect the support sticks, one at a time while staking out the ridge lines.

Bunching along ridgeline

Tom R.: I just put up a poly-tarp in my back yard this weekend. I tried it first the way you described, just drape it over a ridge line and tie the corners down. But I had a big problem with the ridge sagging and bunching up at the ends. I 'fixed' this by creating a tie point on each end of the ridge by bunching up the material and tying a sheet bend to a rope. This is very similar to what you described for making corner ties. Presto! No more sagging ridgeline. I put a lot of tension on it to see if it would break and it's just fine. However it is very ugly and it shortens the tarp by around 10 to 12 inches. Is there a way to somehow attach ridge ties to poly? How about cutting the poly so that each end has a beak-like triangle and then bunch this up. This wouldn't shorten the tarp as much. If you hear news reports about some nut fiddling with plastic sheeting in his back yard it's probably me. Love your books. Keep up the good work!

The bunching is caused by the ridge line sagging between the trees or support sticks. The sagging is caused by any of three factors. One, the ridge line is not tight enough. Two, the type of ridge line chosen is too stretchy, or too thin. Or three, the corner guys are pulling downward with too much tension.

The solution is not to stretch out the ridge by pulling it in opposite directions, but simply to straighten the ridge line. Select a less stretchy material for the line, of a larger diameter so it stretches less. Then tension it tightly. Also insure that the corner guys are not so tight that they pull the ridge downward excessively.

Drip-stopper

Wayne C.: On a canoe camping trip I was co-leading we used a tarp setup. I recall the only problem we encountered was water traveling down (or wicking) along the ridgeline and dripping into the interior of the tarp during rainstorms (we were using nylon parachute cord for our ridgeline). Any suggestions?

Here again, the solution is to eliminate as much of the ridge line sagging as possible, by using stouter cord and tensioning it more tightly. With the line running more horizontal, the rainwater will tend to drip off the line rather than run down it.

Once you have finished pitching the poly-tarp, you may find it difficult to re-tension its ridge line, due to the downward pull of the corner guys. Should drops of rain start flowing down the sagging ridge line and dripping into your living quarters, simply install a make-shift drip-stopper at each end of the tarp, just outside of where the line first meets the tarp.

The drip-stopper is nothing more than a 4-inch length of cord tied tightly around the ridge line. When rainwater runs down the ridge line, it encounters the stopper and drips to the ground there, rather than inside the shelter.

Note that interior dripping does not occur with a ray-way tarp, since its ridgeline does not continue into its interior. The pull loops serve as natural drip-stoppers. Nor is bunching a problem, because the two opposing ridge guys—one at each end—pull the ridge taut.

Internal condensation

Walt S.: I was wondering if the poly-tarps get much condensation? Have enjoyed your books. Thanks.

Some condensation is the result of water vapor given off by the occupants. Beneath an open tarp this is largely wafted away. The remaining condensation is caused by nighttime dew. The amount of dew deposited depends on the humidity and temperature drop. And it depends on what is overhead. Out in the open the dew is heaviest. Many plants, small animals and insects rely on dew for their drinking water. Under the branches of a tree the dew is much reduced. So, pitched beneath tree branches, a tarp will rarely collect dew. Out in the open, the tarp will often collect dew, but since the tarp is overhead, the occupants and their bedding remain dry. Overhead objects minimize or eliminate the dew by blocking radiant heat loss.

Repair of poly-tarp

3-mil polyethylene is quite durable when used with care. But a poly-tarp pitched against a rock, tree or branch could be damaged. Small holes are best repaired with duct tape. Apply the tape to both sides if the damage is more extensive. If you must retire a poly-tarp, consider recycling it by putting it to other uses, for example as a drop cloth or dust cover.

Folding and stowing a poly-tarp

Cory: Just completed my poly-tarp the other day and I'm now out the door to give it a whirl. I also just completed Beyond Backpacking and I wanted to tell you, Ray, how great a read this book is. Certainly changed my thinking in many ways as I'm planning for my AT thru-hike. One thing about the tarp: with the poly am I folding, rolling or stuffing?

In the chapter "At the Tarp Camp" I describe how to stow the ray-way tarp. Much the same method applies to the poly-tarp also.

A combination of folding and rolling works best. Untie the poly-tarp from its anchors, lift the tarp off its ridge line, and fold as you would a blanket, while keeping the air pressed out. Tuck the corner guys between folds to keep them out of the way, then roll into a stowbag-sized bundle.

A stowbag will prevent a wet or dirty tarp from soaking or soiling the contents of your pack or gear bag. But a stowbag is not essential. For many years I carried my tarp in my pack without using a stowbag.

Scouts and poly-tarps

Jim W.: As a Cub Scout leader, I am interested in many aspects of your lightweight hiking approach. Many of our third year cubs are on the small side and carrying the typical backpack, sleeping bag, and tent would tend to overwhelm most of them. Our pack used the poly-tarps this weekend and enjoyed it. The weather was great so we pitched the tarps higher than we would have had we been expecting rain. We did get some rain on Sunday morning and I had to go around and push some feet, sleeping bag ends, and loose gear back under the tarps but the cubs enjoyed the experience. The cubs were both excited and scared by the idea of sleeping under plastic. I think we opened up their eyes to the possibility that you don't need a tent or a cabin to have a good camp.

The poly-tarp is easy to incorporate into Scout outings, and it makes a perfect "hands-on" project while preparing for a campout. Youngsters are typically full of curiosity and will often try new ideas, especially if the leaders show enthusiasm, and time the outings for the best possible conditions.

For a Scout group new to "tarping," the leaders would be wise to pitch a poly-tarp close to home, to familiarize themselves with the process. Then they would devote some time, prior to the actual outing, to teach the scouts about the advantages of the poly-tarp, making the tarps, learning and practicing the knots, learning the 4-point plan of site selection, and actually practicing the pitch. Then on the actual outing, the troop would bring the poly-tarps, and they might also consider backup tents as well. After a review and practice session of knots, site selection and pitching methods, the boys or girls would then band into 4-person tarp-groups, and each group would work together to pitch its shelter. During the learning phase, they would keep the tents handy, but would not actually pitch them unless the weather were to take a turn for the worse. Once the troop has gained confidence in the tarps during one or two such outings, they could leave the tents at home.

For the Scout leaders who take the time to introduce the subject in a straightforward and positive way, the chances are good that the boys or girls will adapt to their poly-tarps quickly and become quite fond of them.

One pointer: avoid taking the scouts tarp camping during the height of mosquito or blackfly season. Even tent camping might not be fun for them at those times.

Karl K.: *I've read Beyond Backpacking, tested your methods at Boy Scout outings, and introduced the Ray-Way of going light to an older Boy Scout contingent bound for a ten-day trek. I am thoroughly pleased with the results!*

You advise in your book and elsewhere to make a gradual transition [from traditional, heavy camping and hiking gear to lightweight gear and methods] and that advice is so accurate. My own 13 year old son is enthusiastic about the functional, packable clothing but his skepticism about the tarp and quilt/pad is only gradually subsiding. It was seeing me use the tarp in conditions of high winds followed by strong rains that began to convince him. One or two tents in our group leaked while I and a tarpmate remained high and dry. Not-so-young adults coming on these outings seem to really enjoy the tarp, even when they have to bend down more to get in and out. It is comfortable, made of interesting material, with far less condensation and "it works".

"Improvements"

Bob M.: I am just finishing the poly-tarp and intend to use it on the Superior Hiking Trail. (If you have not been here, you should try it. It's a good walk along Lake Superior.) We are in serious bug country here especially in the spring. What can I do to make the shelter more bug proof? Can I hang no-see-um mesh under the tarp in some way? Thank you Ray for these how-to's.

Hanging no-see-um mesh under the poly-tarp is unlikely to be effective, for reasons described elsewhere in this book. If you do not want to make a net-tent, you could wear mosquito-proof clothing at night, including a headnet, and perhaps cover your face with an additional piece of no-see-um netting for the night.

Charles: I cut the corners of the tarp to a V-shape, making sheet bend knots easy to tie.

Cutting the corners of the tarp to a V-shape would stress the tarp enormously where their edges converge at the center. For best results, use a rectangular piece of material, and tie the double sheet bend knots in each corner only once. Leave the corner guys attached to the poly-tarp for the life of the tarp. What could be easier?

Kash: I've been messing with poly-tarps for a while now and use an iron to weld seams in them. Once you get the knack, they're smooth and as strong as the material itself. The extra heavy duty clear plastic that furniture comes wrapped in is a really useful material. You'll need to lay paper between the plastic and the iron to buffer the heat or the plastic will melt to the iron's sole. You also need to use thicker layers on either side of the seam to make the edges of the welded area more regular. Once you're finished with the iron, fold the excess back over the seam and trim the excess with a razor by sliding it underneath so as not to nick into the tarp's surface. I've made a few tarps this way and like your beaked design. I think my next one will also have pockets in the edges to fill with rocks to hold them down in wind as you've described.

Hal W.: *I used 2 mil to save weight. I reinforced the corners and the points where the line emerges on the front and back of the peak with another layer of 2 mil, attached with double-sided exterior carpet tape. I then put grommets at the corners and put a small loop of thin shock cord through the grommets. When putting up the tarp, the stakes go through the loops of shock cord. In high wind, the tarp never gets much stress, due to the give in the shock cord. Rocks can be put on the shock cord to weigh down the edges of the tarp without punching holes in it.*

I like these ideas, not particularly for their methods, but their innovative approach. This kind of experimentation can sometimes lead, through trial and error, to new and useful ideas. At the same time, I would caution anyone about trusting novel ideas not backed by years of experience. Ideas such as these two might sound promising, but would they hold up in a storm?

A strong wind will almost certainly rip out grommets, despite reinforcements and shock cord. The double sheet bend is many times stronger, although perhaps not as trendy.

Polyethylene (or silicone-nylon) is inherently elastic and my recommended 3-mil poly is capable of absorbing much of the shock loading from strong wind gusts. But what concerns us most with these thin-laminate tarps is the aerodynamic loading. This is a function of surface area presentation, and shock cord does nothing to reduce aero loading. The way we reduce aero loading is by pitching the tarp low-lying, giving it a smaller wind profile. (Something we cannot do with a tent.) With 3-mil material, sheet bend knots, and a low pitch with solid anchor points, the poly-tarp will stay put in very strong wind. Especially if pitched behind natural protection.

In high winds we would pitch the poly-tarp quite low to the ground, with its sides lying against the ground and stretched very tightly by the corner guys to keep them there. No matter what the wind, there is none on the ground. This effect is known as "wind gradient." The closer to the ground, the less wind—due to ground friction. So if the tarp sides are on the ground and stretched tightly, they will tend to stay there regardless of how strong the wind is blowing.

In extremely strong wind one could rock the edges down. Use smooth rocks to avoid tearing the plastic material. Do not try this with a nylon tarp, because it is not as tough as polyethylene. Alternatively, one could add side guys (not corner guys which are highly stressed) using Hal's method: double-sided tape, reinforcement patches, and shock cord onto which the rocks would lie. But again, I have a great deal of experience with poly-tarps in extremely stiff wind, and have not found the need for side guys.

Scott S.: *Thanks for the ideas and the inspiration. I am an outdoor enthusiast and a Scout Leader, and am always looking for fresh ideas for myself, as well as the boys. This could make a great troop project, and fun for me! I'll let you know how it goes.*

Joe W.: *Loved Beyond Backpacking so I took a minute to build a poly-tarp this week and I can't get over how flexible it is to pitch and take down compared to my ultra-expensive "no-hitch-pitch" tent. I'm amazed at how I have gotten off the common-sense path and complicated things in life. You've made me a believer!*

Ken C.: *My children love to play and sleep under the poly-tarp we made together.*

Joe G.: *I made a single person poly-tarp and used it for a weekend trip. No tent can compare to the luxurious roominess, total ventilation and real, substantial weight savings afforded by a tarp!! My only regret is that I didn't trust you on the thickness. I figured that if 3 mil was good, 4 mil would be better. While the thicker poly is stronger, I soon found that it is unnecessarily so. Consequently, it was heavier and more opaque. While playing with some scraps, I was amazed at how much force is needed to deform the poly with a sheet-bend knot, certainly much more than even a gale force wind could deliver!*

Charlie D.: *One of the most exciting things about the poly-tarp: IT'S SO EASY! They are so much fun, I've made three of them. They are amazingly sturdy, and they cost next to nothing*

Ray-Way Sewing Projects: Getting started

Sewing your own tarp, net-tent and stowbags can save you money over buying them commercially. And the sewing is not difficult, even for someone with little or no sewing experience. All it takes is a small investment in your time. This is quality time, working with your hands to produce something that will serve you well in the wilds. And I have always felt that home-made gear actually outperforms commercial gear, especially when customized to your specific needs. Certainly it is far more meaningful, something you can be truly proud of.

I have organized the sewing material sequentially, in eight chapters:

• This first short chapter, Getting Started, covers the rudiments of sewing.

• The next chapter describes the materials.

• Then we proceed to cutting out the pieces for the ray-way tarp and stowbags.

• Next comes another short chapter on adjusting the sewing machine.

• After that comes a pair of practice projects: stowbags for tarp and stakes.

• Then a short chapter on sewing the flat-felled seam.

• Then, step-by-step instructions for sewing a ray-way tarp.

• And lastly, sewing a net-tent.

I hope my enthusiasm for the tarp, net-tent and stowbags will help motivate you to make them for yourself. It all starts with a sewing machine and a desire to create these worthwhile projects.

The sewing machine

The fabrics used to make a tarp and net-tent are relatively light and easy to sew. A simple home-type sewing machine, even with only the most basic features, can produce excellent results. To create the projects in this book, your machine need sew only two types of stitches:

1) The straight stitch, used for sewing all the seams and hems.

2) The reverse stitch, used to terminate each row of straight stitching, simply by sewing backward about half an inch. This prevents the straight stitch from raveling, or coming apart.

Most home-type sewing machines can also sew a zigzag stitch. This stitch is not essential for the projects in this book, though you could use it in a few places, as mentioned in the instructions. The zigzag is quite useful for sewing outdoor garments made of stretch fabrics. By nature of its geometry, it expands like an accordion when the material is stretched.

Most older sewing machines contain metal parts primarily, and tend to be more robust and powerful than their modern, plastic counterparts. And because these older machines lack the computerized wizardry, they are often more reliable. I have seen useable old machines going for as little as $25 in second hand stores. Of course, not all old machines are in good working order. But if you find one that seems to have prospects, perhaps you could try sewing with it right there in the store. If it will produce a stitch that is even both top and bottom, as described below, chances are it will serve your needs very well.

Most retail sewing machine stores listed in your phone book also sell used sewing machines. These machines are normally inspected, and refurbished where necessary; and they are under warranty. Moreover, the salespeople are usually knowledgably, and can demonstrate the machine to assure you it is operating correctly.

Or someone in your family might have a sewing machine that you could borrow.

Needles

Needles are an often-overlooked detail. But they become worn and damaged with use, especially when sewing synthetic fabrics, which tend to be more abrasive to the needle than cotton. The wear or damage to a needle is rarely apparent to the eye, but it can cause all sorts of problems with the sewing. A dull or damaged needle will skip stitches or damage thread, and is often indicated by a clicking or popping sound each time the needle penetrates the fabric. Other baffling and frustrating problems can result from the needle tip burring or blunting, microscopic nicks, or a bent shank. So for best results, begin each project with a new, high-quality needle.

Look for sewing machine needles at fabric stores or large department stores that sell sewing supplies.

The projects detailed in this book call for metric size 80 needles (US size 12), or size 90 (14), your choice. If you can find small shank, "sharp," then use those. Otherwise, "Universal" and ballpoints usually suffice.

Thread

The thread that Jenny and I use on all our sewing projects is a type of continuous fiber polyester. This thread sews better and yields more consistent seams. We like it so much that we offer it in the line of Ray-Way Products. Medium weight 100% long-fiber polyester thread, available at sewing stores, would also suffice for these projects. As a last resort, one could use cotton-covered polyester thread. Nylon thread would be a poor choice, because it is less resistant to UV-b deterioration.

Thread color is your choice, but is often limited by availability. Optimally, the thread would match the fabric. Contrasting thread colors is another option. And black is a universal thread color that goes well on most outdoor projects.

Notions

In addition to the needles, thread, and fabric, a few sewing notions can facilitate the marking, cutting and sewing. These include:

• Small safety pins.

• Box of plastic-coated paperclips.

• Small box of straight pins.

• Seam ripper, sometimes called a stitch picker.

• Fine-point permanent marker, black seems to work best.

• Tape measure.

• Wooden or plastic yardstick and ruler.

• Sharp scissors.

• Candle for searing the edges of webbing and ends of cord.

Ray-Way Kits

Many home sewing enthusiasts have found that the only real difficulty in making the ray-way tarp and net-tent has been locating the recommended fabrics, cord and miscellaneous hardware. Various fabric and sewing supply outlets list their wares in catalogs and on the Internet. But while these companies try to maintain a wide stock, rarely can they meet the requirements of the highly specialized ray-way gear.

As a result, many people have made ray-way projects using materials that are sub-standard, and in some cases completely unsuitable. This is unfortunate because these projects rely on the materials for best performance.

To remedy the situation, I am providing kits for my tarp and net-tent. These kits reflect my own philosophy and practice of using only the finest and most appropriate materials. Using these kits while following the instructions in this book, you can create a tarp and net-tent that are virtually identical to the ones that Jenny and I make and use. And not only that, but the kits will save you time searching for the right materials elsewhere, and they will save you money.

Please check our web site for availability, color and materials options, prices, ordering information and new products:

Ray-Way Products

www.ray-way.com

email: rayway@isp01.net

P.O. Box 2153 Arizona City, AZ 85223

Thread

In addition to the kits, we are also selling what we consider the world's finest sewing thread, certainly far superior to that sold in stores. It has continuous fibers that are soft and very smooth. So it is less fuzzy than ordinary long-fiber polyester thread, and more resistant to sun rot. With this thread the seams are easier to sew, with fewer problems and less frequent cleaning and maintenance of the machine required. This thread is ideal for use in virtually all camping-related home sewing projects.

Contents of the Ray-Way Tarp Kit

The ray-way tarp kit will make either a one-person tarp, or a two-person tarp. The kit contains the following items:

Tarp fabric: silicone-nylon

The fabric I recommend for most camping situations is the lightweight silicone-coated nylon, sometimes called silicone-impregnated nylon. Technically, it is a silicone-elastomer coating applied to both sides of ripstop nylon. Both sides are equally coated and essentially the same; neither side is differentiated as top or bottom.

This particular nylon, before coating, is 1.1 ounces per square yard. After coating it is around 1.3 oz/yd². As with any fabric, this refers to the weight in ounces of one square yard of fabric.

This particular material is thinner than urethane-nylon, so it stretches more in high wind. And it requires more careful handling in the field.

The type of silicone-nylon sold by many fabric outlets is "seconds" grade. The usual reason for this classification is that the material is flawed in certain areas, usually the coating. These flaws are often subtle in appearance, and most customers hardly notice them, until their tarps leak during the first rainstorm.

My tarp kits contain only first quality silicone-nylon.

Tarp fabric: urethane-nylon

Alternatively, we also sell tarp kits containing urethane-coated nylon. Again, this is first quality fabric only, no "seconds."

This material, prior to coating, is 1.9 ounces per square yard. After coating it is around 2.7 oz/yd². And since both the nylon and coating are heavier than the silicone-nylon, the material stretches less. Urethane-nylon might be the preferred choice for someone who frequently camps in high winds.

Also this material is more durable, at least when not exposed to prolonged sun. The urethane-nylon tarp that Jenny and I used on our 1994 PCT hike is over fifteen years old and still in good shape; we continue to use it occasionally.

With a urethane-nylon tarp, the shiny side is the coated side, and it goes toward the earth. The uncoated side goes toward the sky. This protects the coating from the sun's UV-b. This still leaves the uncoated side exposed, but since the material is about twice as sun-resistant as the coating, this seems to be the best compromise.

By the way, please note that nearly all coated nylons are flammable. Note also that the fire-retardant chemicals often added to commercial backpacking tents can be detrimental to one's health.

Webbing

The webbing contained in the tarp kit is the specific webbing I recommend for the pull loops. It has the optimum thickness and width, and the best flexibility providing the highest strength and best stowability, while still being as lightweight as possible.

Guy lines

The selection of guy lines in these kits is the best available anywhere. For example, the tarp corner guys are 1/16 inch diameter and 250 lb test! The ridge guys are a stouter 1/8 inch diameter, and the side, beak and lifter guys are a specialized flat line carefully chosen for its subtle stiffness, greatly reducing tangles.

Cord locks

Not all cord locks are created equal. These kits contain first quality cord locks of the appropriate size for the ray-way projects.

Stowbag materials

The kit also contains the fabric, drawstring cord and cord locks needed to make a tarp stowbag and a stakes stowbag.

Contents of the Net-tent Kit

The net-tent kit will make either a one-person net-tent or a two-person model, and the materials are equally high caliber. The kit contains no-see-um netting for the roof, side walls, headwall and footwall; silicone-nylon for the floor, and all the suspension lines, reinforcement material, cord locks and suspension hooks. Additionally, the kit contains enough silicone-nylon for making a net-tent stowbag.

The cord locks included with this kit (for the adjustable suspension lines) are so small and lightweight that many people will find them amazing. Each is a mere .55" long, and weighs a scant .02 ounce. And yet these little units grab the line with surprising tenacity.

Tarp colors

I think most campers would agree that a hot pink or neon-colored tarp would be out of place in the wilderness. A silver-colored aluminized one would likewise be a glaring standout.

A bright and light colored tarp, such as white and bright yellow or gold, can be very glaring as we lie beneath it, at least while the sun is shining brightly.

In terms of performance, black is another undesirable color. Even though darker colors are more sun resistant, black or dark fabric absorbs more heat by day and radiates, or loses, more by night.

Also, contrary to expectations, black is visible at night. Once your eyes have adjusted to the darkness, you will see that nothing out there is naturally black. So a black tarp stands out as something out of place.

The best colors in terms of low profile camping are those that more closely match the surroundings. Natural, subdued colors such as pale sky blue, and earth tones like tan, brown, grey and subtle forest green help a tarp blend with the wilds. You and your camp remain unobtrusive and unnoticed, and this provides more security and sense of privacy.

Cutting the Pieces for Tarp and Stowbags

This chapter assumes that you have a sewing machine, fresh needles, polyester thread, and that you have purchased a ray-way tarp kit. Here, we will cut out the pieces for the tarp and stowbags. With the left-over scraps, we will proceed to the next chapter and learn to adjust the sewing machine for an even, balanced stitch. Once you feel comfortable sewing practice seams, the succeeding chapter will show you how to make a small stowbag for your tarp stakes, and another stowbag for your ray-way tarp. These simple projects will give you the skill and confidence needed to begin sewing your tarp.

Measure and cut out the panels

The instructions that follow are for marking and cutting the panels and pieces for a two-person ray-way tarp with beaks. If you are making a one-person tarp, simply refer to the smaller dimensions given in parentheses.

Note that if you would like to shave a few ounces from your finished tarp, you could taper the panels, making them narrower at the foot, and reduce the size of the foot beak accordingly. Such a tarp you would pitch somewhat lower at the foot end. However, the rectangular shape offers the best coverage, and despite its somewhat greater weight I feel it is the best option for those with little or no tarp experience. The instructions in these chapters are for making a rectangular tarp.

The fabric in a ray-way tarp kit is a rectangle. Meaning that its ends are perpendicular to its sides. If you buy material elsewhere, the ends are unlikely to be perpendicular, and you may have to trim them to make them true.

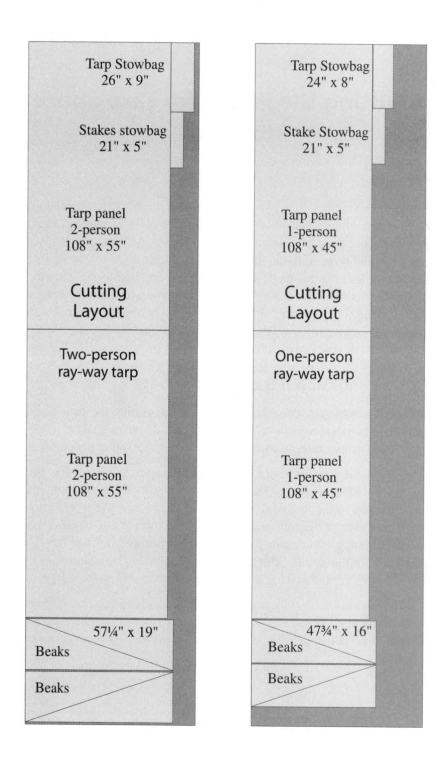

Tarp Stowbag
26" x 9"

Stakes stowbag
21" x 5"

Tarp panel
2-person
108" x 55"

Cutting
Layout

Two-person
ray-way tarp

Tarp panel
2-person
108" x 55"

57¼" x 19"

Beaks

Beaks

Tarp Stowbag
24" x 8"

Stake Stowbag
21" x 5"

Tarp panel
1-person
108" x 45"

Cutting
Layout

One-person
ray-way tarp

Tarp panel
1-person
108" x 45"

47¾" x 16"

Beaks

Beaks

Begin by laying out the fabric on a clean, flat surface. A freshly vacuumed carpet or mopped floor would work fine, even if it is not seven yards long.

Looking closely at the tarp fabric, you will notice that the two lengthwise edges are "finished." The widthwise (warp) threads do not terminate at the fabric edge. Rather, they turn 180 degrees and re-enter the fabric. In sewing terminology, this type of edge is known as a "selvage."

From the kit material you will begin by cutting two panels 108 inches in length.

Place a measuring tape along one selvage, and use a fine-point permanent marker to make a small tick 108 inches from one end.

Place the measuring tape along the opposite selvage, and tick that at 108 inches.

Lay the tape across the fabric from one tick to the other, and using the tape as a straight edge, make a few more ticks. Use a yardstick to draw a line along the ticks. Then with a pair of scissors cut along the line.

Mark and cut out a second panel of the same size.

These two panels will form the tarp body. Each panel is 108 inches long. Now, trim both pieces to 55 inches wide (45 inches for a one-person tarp).

Each panel now measures 108" by 55" (108" x 45" for a one-person tarp). Fold them carefully and set aside.

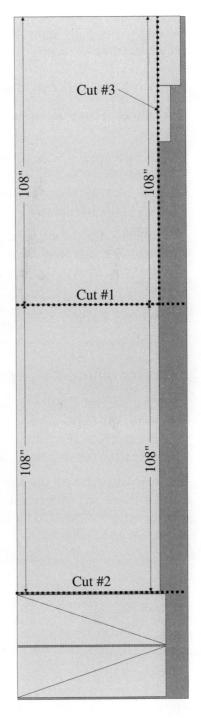

Note that because of the coating, you will not need to heat-seal the raw edges, especially since the seams and perimeter hem will envelop and protect the raw edges.

Measure and cut out the beaks

Three pieces of material remain. Two are long and narrow; the third is full width.

Using the piece that is full width, cut two rectangles each measuring 57¼ inches by 19 inches (47¾" x 16" for a one-person tarp). Draw a diagonal line through each rectangle, extending from one corner to the diagonally opposite corner.

Note that the two diagonal lines traverse the rectangles in opposite directions. One runs from the top left corner to the bottom right corner. The other runs from the bottom left corner to the top right corner.

Cut along the diagonal lines. This makes four triangles, with which you will later make the beaks.

Fold the four triangles and set them aside.

Beaks for different size panels

My recommended sizes may seem quite large. But they are based on experience with tarps in strong wind and rain. During a storm you need the ample coverage. If you decide to make your tarp smaller, to save weight, remember that your shelter will also be less storm-worthy.

To make a different size tarp, or to taper your tarp panels, refer to the table for the correct beak rectangle size. PW is the panel width. W is the beak triangle width; and L is the beak triangle length. These measurements include the seam allowances.

If your desired panel width is not listed in the table, use the formulas.

Beak rectangles for various tarp panel widths							
PW	55	54	53	52	51	50	49	48
W	19	18-3/4	18-1/2	18-1/4	17-3/4	17-1/2	17-1/4	16-3/4
L	57-1/4	56-1/4	55-1/4	54-1/2	53-1/2	52-1/2	51-1/2	50-1/2

PW	47	46	45	44	43	42	41	40
W	16-1/2	16-1/4	16	15-1/2	15-1/4	15	14-3/4	14-1/4
L	49-3/4	48-3/4	47-3/4	46-3/4	45-3/4	45	44	43

$$W = PW * .316 + 1.685$$
$$L = PW * .947 + 5.055$$

Measure and cut the stowbags

From one of the long, narrow scraps, you can now mark and cut out a pair of stowbags: one for the stakes, the other for the tarp. I recommend you make these stowbags first, for practice sewing, before making the tarp.

Mark and cut a rectangle measuring 26 inches by 9 inches (24" x 8" for a one-person tarp). This will be your tarp stowbag. Set it aside.

The stake stowbag (which will hold up to 12 rod type stakes about 7 inches long) uses a rectangle 21 inches by 5 inches. Mark that and cut it out. Set these two pieces aside.

The remaining pieces are scraps. Some you will use to adjust your sewing machine and practice various types of seams and stitches. The rest you might use later for making other stowbags, etc. Additionally, you will make a pair of small reinforcement patches for the tarp, and these we will discuss in the tarp sewing instructions.

Adjusting the Sewing Machine

For a machine to sew correctly, it must be properly threaded and adjusted. And proper adjustment depends on the type and thickness of thread and material sewn. So I will describe how to adjust your machine while sewing a few scraps of silicone-nylon.

Three points to keep in mind:

The most common error for both beginner and more experienced is using a worn or damaged needle. This can cause all sorts of baffling problems with the stitching. Always begin each new project with a new needle.

The second most common error is incorrect top threading. In other words, the path the thread follows from the spool, through the bales and tensioning wheel, to the needle.

The third most common error is incorrect bobbin threading.

The manual for your sewing machine describes bobbin winding, top and bobbin threading and adjusting, and so forth. If you do not have such a manual, you can probably obtain a copy from a sewing machine store.

Adjusting bobbin tension

Before you begin sewing, check the bobbin tension. Remove the bobbin along with its case, and make this simple test: Grasp the thread extending from the bobbin and case, and with it, try to lift the two. If the thread slips out so easily that it cannot lift bobbin and case, then tighten the set-screw slightly. Conversely, if the thread easily lifts the bobbin and its case, then loosen the set-screw slightly.

A properly adjusted bobbin and case will barely hang from the thread, and a slight jouncing will cause them to descend.

Balancing the stitch

Cut a few 6-inch squares of silicone-nylon from your scraps. Set your machine to sew a medium straight stitch, 10 to 12 stitches per inch. Make sure the needle is all the way up. Lift the presser foot, place the two scraps into the sewing area, and lower the presser foot onto them.

Note: As you begin to sew a new seam, you must immobilize the upper and bobbin threads by holding them firmly between thumb and index finger, or by pressing them against the sewing surface with a finger. This prevents the machinery from pulling these threads down into the bobbin case. After the first few stitches you can let go.

Sew two pieces of material together and examine the stitches on the upper and lower surfaces.

Are the stitches reasonably similar, both top and bottom? If so, then the stitches are correctly linked midway between the two layers of fabric. This is what we refer to as a "balanced" stitch.

On the other hand, if the stitches on one surface are different than those on the other, then the settings require adjustment.

Re-examine the thread on both surfaces of the test pieces. Is there more thread apparent on the bottom than the top? (Upper thread visible on lower surface.) If yes, then increase the machine's upper tension by turning the tension wheel to a higher number.

If there is more thread on top, then decrease the upper tension.

After each adjustment, sew a new line of stitches across your test pieces, and examine the stitches.

Sewing an even stitch

A balanced stitch looks the same on both sides. An even stitch is straight and clean with no puckers or skipped stitches. If you have begun with a new needle, threaded the machine and bobbin holder properly, adjusted the bobbin tension and the upper tension, and still the machine will not sew an even, balanced stitch, then the machine may require cleaning and servicing. Sometimes a person will exert too much force on the wheel while trying to clear a jam. This can slip the timing, and is something that only a technician can adjust.

If the stitch looks like this on both sides,

it is properly balanced.

If the stitch looks like this on the upper surface,

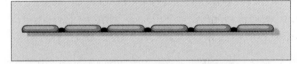

the lower threads are being pulled through
by too much upper tension.

Foot pressure

Some machines adjust the foot pressure automatically, while other machines allow you to adjust the foot pressure manually. Lighter materials require lighter foot pressure. And indeed, silicone-nylon is quite light. Excessive foot pressure is indicated by the lower piece of material shoving ahead of the upper piece.

Seam allowance

Let's assume, now, that your machine is operating correctly.

With two new scraps, line up the edges and sew a row of stitches half an inch from the right edges. This half-inch margin between the edge and the stitches is called the "seam allowance." Different projects require different seam allowances, but the tarp, net-tent and stowbags use ½".

Avoid the temptation of trimming the seam allowances to nearly nothing in an attempt to save weight and bulk. A wide seam allowance gives your projects much greater durability and longevity. The stitches need the extra fabric beyond them for optimum strength.

Backstitch

When sewing a line of stitches, always backstitch half an inch at the start and at the finish of the seam. Backstitching reinforces the seam at each end by preventing the threads from pulling free. Here is how it is done:

Begin sewing at the edge, and sew only ½". Stop, and reverse the sewing direction on your sewing machine from forward to reverse, by pressing a button, or turning a dial or lever. Sew backwards ½" over the initial stitching. Then reverse the direction again to the forward stitch, and proceed to sew the entire seam. At the end of the seam, repeat this backstitching process.

Sewing tips

• For best accuracy, sew slowly. And stop frequently to shift and guide the fabrics as they feed into the needle.

• Let the machine do the work. Use your hands only to guide the material, while resisting the temptation to pull or push.

• To change direction abruptly, lower the needle to its down position using the hand wheel, lift the presser foot, rotate the material around the needle, lower the presser foot, and resume sewing.

• You can improvise a sewing guide by applying a piece of adhesive tape to the throat plate, (the horizontal plate under the needle) the appropriate distance from the needle.

Ray-Way Stowbags

This chapter describes how to make a pair of ray-way stowbags, one for a set of stakes and the other for the tarp. Each stowbag is made from a single piece of coated nylon, folded at the bottom and sewn along each side, with a turned-down collar that creates a casing for a draw cord.

Jenny and I designed these stowbags to be simple to construct, yet more refined than most produced commercially. We hope you enjoy making and using them.

Stake stowbag

In this project we will use the 21-inch by 5-inch rectangle coated nylon, cut in a previous chapter.

Marking

Lay the piece of material on your sewing table, with one of the short ends toward you. From the upper right and left corners, mark the fabric at 1½ inches and 3 inches from the top. On the left side only, make an additional mark at 2 inches. Each of these marks should be about ¾" in length.

Mark the other end the same way.

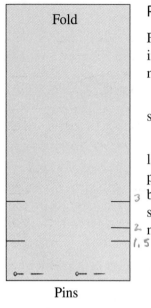

Fold

Pins

Pinning

Fold the material in half, forming a 10½ by 5-inch rectangle. The marks at both ends should now coincide.

Insure the edges are aligned, then insert two straight-pins near the nearest edge.

To insert a straight-pin, push it through both layers of fabric, then re-direct it and continue pushing it back out, as illustrated. This leaves both the head and point of the pin on the same side of the fabric, separated by a quarter-inch of material.

Pinning will prevent the layers from shifting as you sew them together. Always pin on the seam allowance, never on the body of the project where the pin holes would be visible and possibly leak. The seam allowances for the stowbags are ½".

Next, insert three more pins along the right edge.

Note that by aligning pins with their heads toward you, you can easily remove each pin as it reaches the sewing machine needle.

½"

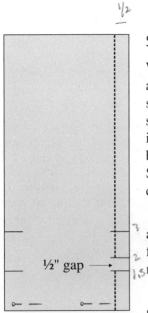

½" gap →

Sewing the first seam

Doesn't this Leave raw edge exposed? (handwritten)

We will now sew the two halves together, half an inch from the right edge. To begin, we will sew a line of stitching starting at the fold, and stopping at the middle of the three marks (which is 2" from the end). Backstitch an inch at the beginning. At the second mark, backstitch twice. Stop all stitching at the second mark, without crossing it.

Now sew another line of stitching beginning at the third mark (1½" from the end) and finishing at the end. Back stitch twice at the third mark, and once at the end.

Again, remove each pin as it reaches the sewing machine needle.

We have now sewn the two halves together along their right edge, leaving a ½" seam allowance, and leaving a ½" gap between the second and third marks.

Remove all remaining pins.

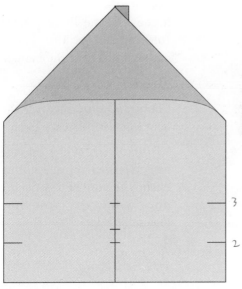

Open the material by spreading the two halves from their right sides. Lay the piece flat on the sewing table, as shown.

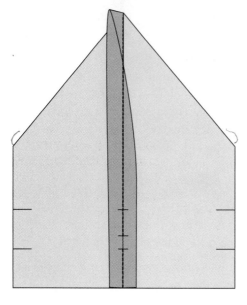

Turn the piece over, spread the seam allowance edges on the lower half of the piece, and press the allowances flat.

Crease the folds by running your thumbnail over them. This is called "finger pressing," and is a very useful technique when sewing silicone-coated nylon.

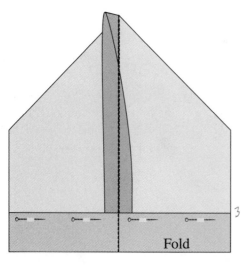

Fold

Fold the bottom edge to the highest of the three marks, forming a 1½" draw cord casing. Finger press this fold.

The seam allowance for the hem stitch will be ¼".

Insert a few pins into the hem to prevent it from shifting during sewing. Position the pins within ¼" from the material's edge.

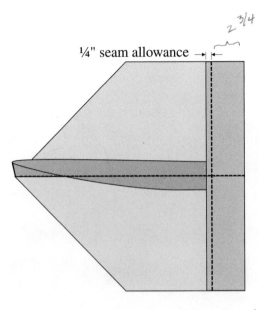

¼" seam allowance

Sewing the casing

Place the piece into the sewing machine, and stitch the casing along its full length, leaving a seam allowance of ¼".

Sewing the second side seam

Fold the piece in half lengthwise, with the casing on the outside. Pin together.

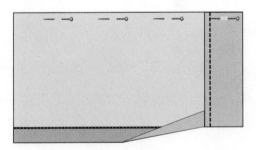

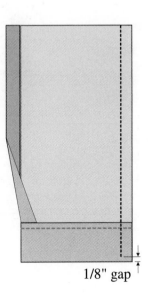

Sew the second side seam, with a ½" seam allowance. But stop short of the casing fold, leaving a 1/8" gap. Back stitch at both ends of the seam.

1/8" gap

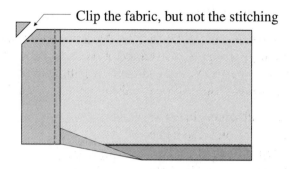

Clip the fabric, but not the stitching

With a pair of scissors, trim the corner on a diagonal, close to the stitching without actually cutting the stitching.

The sewing of this project is complete. Turn the stowbag right-side out. Next you will install a draw cord.

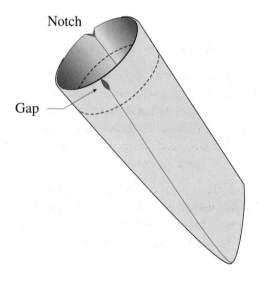

Notch

Gap

Installing the draw cord

Because the stowbag is so small and light, the draw cord must be thin and light also. From your supply of cord, cut a piece 14 inches long. If the cord contains core filaments, remove them by pulling them out one end. Discard the filaments, and melt both ends of the draw cord lightly.

Attach a small safety pin to one end of the draw cord, and feed it into the stitching gap, through the casing half way around, through the small notch cut out on the diagonal, continuing through the casing back to the entry point, and back out the stitching gap.

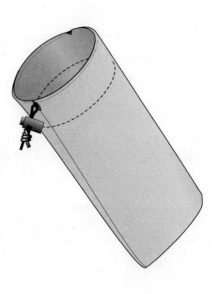

Remove the safety pin, and install a cord lock. Then open the stowbag fully and position the cord lock half an inch from the bag. Tie an overhand knot in the ends of the doubled cord, and work the knot toward the cord lock until nearly touching it. Trim the excess cord and melt the ends lightly.

Congratulations! Your stowbag is finished.

If your stowbag did not turn out as nicely as you had hoped, perhaps due to mistakes or inaccurate sewing, take heart. The reason we started with the small, stake stowbag is that it uses very little material. So if you are not happy with your first stowbag, you have plenty of scraps to start over and make another one. Your next stowbag will go together quicker because you now understand the process.

Once you have made a stake stowbag to your satisfaction, then you are ready to sew your tarp stowbag. These projects are mainly for practice, to familiarize you with the sewing techniques before starting your tarp. So be patient, and do not be tempted to take shortcuts.

Where are dimensions?

Tarp stowbag

The tarp stowbag is sewn in the same way as the stake stowbag. The only differences are the dimensions of the material and the length of draw cord: 23 inches for a two-person tarp stowbag, and 21 inches for a one-person. In a previous chapter you cut the silicone nylon piece out. So go ahead and sew your tarp stowbag now, referring to the drawings for the stake stowbag where necessary.

When sewing stowbags of any shape and size, remember to make the draw cord casings at least as wide as those shown here. This allows the draw cord to close and open the bag with minimal effort.

23" x 5" 2 person
21 x 5' 1 Person or stake bag

The Flat-Felled Seam

The flat-felled seam is easy to sew, and it envelops and protects the raw edges while lending a finished appearance to your project.

Both the tarp and net-tent use flat-felled seams. When learning to sew this seam, practice with a pair of scraps measuring about 6 by 12 inches. Place the uncoated, less shiny sides together for urethane-coated nylon; either way for silicone-nylon.

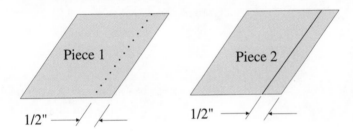

Piece 1   Piece 2

1/2"   1/2"

Half an inch from the edge of one piece, make a series of dots with a fine-point permanent marker. On large pieces such as tarp panels, make the dots every 6 or 8 inches along the length of material.

Repeat on the other piece of material, but this time connect the dots by drawing a continuous line, guided by a ruler or yardstick.

These two reference lines, one dotted and the other continuous, will help maintain alignment as you sew the initial row of stitching. Ultimately the marks will be hidden inside the seam.

Lay the second piece on top of the first, but offset them by half an inch, such that the edge of the top piece lies on the dotted line of the bottom piece. The solid line on the top piece will serve as your stitching guide.

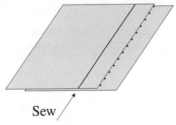

Sew

Thus positioned, the seam allowance of the top piece will be half an inch, and the bottom piece, one inch.

Pin the two pieces together along their seam allowances. This will prevent them from shifting as you sew.

Stitch along the solid line, removing each pin as it reaches the needle.

Fold the bottom, one-inch seam allowance over the top half-inch seam allowance. Fold both down, finger press, and sew only about three inches. Keep repeating the process along the full length of the seam.

Lay the two pieces of fabric on the sewing table, one on top of the other, uncoated (less shiny) sides together.

The seam allowance (to the right of the stitch) is ½" on the upper piece, and 1" on the lower.

Stitch

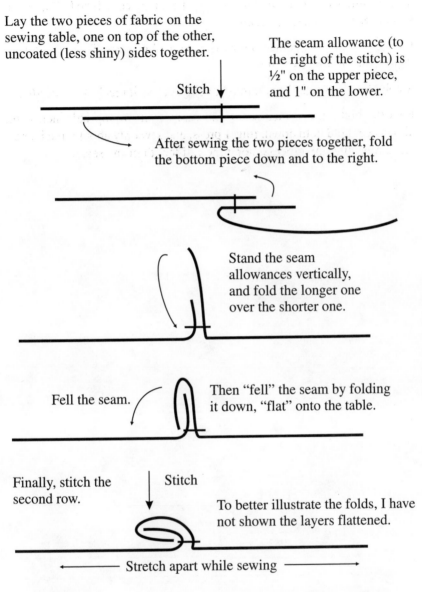

After sewing the two pieces together, fold the bottom piece down and to the right.

Stand the seam allowances vertically, and fold the longer one over the shorter one.

Fell the seam.

Then "fell" the seam by folding it down, "flat" onto the table.

Finally, stitch the second row.

Stitch

To better illustrate the folds, I have not shown the layers flattened.

Stretch apart while sewing

Position this stitch as far to the left as practical. If the needle misses the middle layer, that would not be a problem.

Seam-seal this side

Sewing a Ray-Way Tarp

The ray-way tarp is a simple and straightforward home-sewing project, even for someone with little sewing experience. If you have followed the previous chapters and successfully completed their projects, you are ready to begin the tarp. This chapter provides step by step instructions accompanied with numerous illustrations. I suggest you read the chapter through, then return to this point and begin the actual construction.

Construction steps, in summary:

1. You will begin by sewing the two roof panels together using a flat-felled seam, then adding a pair of reinforcement pieces. Then you will:

2. Sew the beak-halves together; then the beaks to the tarp.

3. Stitch ridge pull-loops in place.

4. Sew a perimeter hem.

5. Stitch the remaining pull loops, lifter patches and utility loops in place.

6. Attach the guys with simple knots.

7. And lastly, you will seam seal the ridge and beaks.

Sewing the ridge seam

The tarp body is made from the two panels that you cut out, as directed in an earlier chapter. While following the previous chapter, you practiced sewing a flat-felled seam. This is the type of seam you will now use to join the two panels.

Urethane-nylon is coated on one side only, identified by its higher sheen (more shiny). If making your tarp of this material, place the two panels on the floor, one on top of the other, with their uncoated (less shiny) sides together. The finished tarp will then have its uncoated sides toward the sky, and its coated sides toward the ground. This protects the coating from the sun's UV-b.

Silicone-nylon is coated on both sides equally. If making your tarp of this material, place the two panels on the floor, one on top of the other in no particular order.

Examine the two panels and locate their selvage edges. These edges will go into the flat-felled seam, which then becomes the tarp's ridge.

Turn the top panel to align its selvage with that of the bottom panel.

One panel at a time, mark a half-inch seam allowance along the selvage edge, just as you did on the smaller practice pieces. That is, the bottom panel receives a dotted line, while the top panel receives a solid line; and each line is ½" from its selvage.

Position the top panel so that its selvage lies directly on the dotted line of the bottom panel.

Pin the two panels together along their full length, spacing the pins about 6" apart and keeping them inside the seam allowance.

With the panels pinned together, position them at your sewing machine and sew a straight stitch along the full length of the solid line. Again, the solid line is half an inch from the top panel's selvage, and one inch from the bottom panel's selvage. Be sure to backstitch at the start of the seam, and again at its end.

Finish the flat-felled seam by spreading the panels, tucking the seam allowance over and down, and sewing in place as explained in the previous chapter.

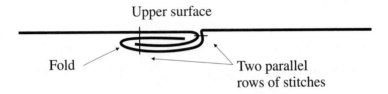

Upper surface

Fold — Two parallel rows of stitches

Identifying top and bottom

In the instructions that follow, you will need to know which side of the tarp is the upper surface, facing the sky, and which side is the lower surface, facing the ground. One side of the flat-felled seam is smooth. The other side has a short fold of material extending beyond one row of stitching. This fold is on the tarp's lower surface.

Ridge reinforcements

Next, you will make a pair of reinforcement patches, and sew them to the tarp's lower surface, one at each end of the ridge.

On a piece of scrap, of the same type of material as your tarp, measure, mark, and cut two isosceles triangles (triangles with two equal sides) each having a base of 7 inches and a height of 3½ inches. Fold each side of the triangle under itself a quarter inch. Do not fold the base. Finger press both folds. Then pin the folds to the triangle itself, and sew the folds to the triangle.

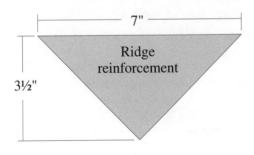

7"

Ridge reinforcement

3½"

Lay the tarp on your sewing table, with the tarp's lower surface facing up. At one end of the ridge, position a reinforcement triangle in the following way:

• Base of the triangle flush with the end of the tarp panels.

• Apex of the triangle centered on the ridge flat-felled seam.

• Both side folds tucked under the triangle.

Pin the triangle to the tarp, to hold it in place.

Starting at the triangle's apex, stitch to the base along one side, then the other side. Backstitch at the apex only. Do not sew along the triangle's base.

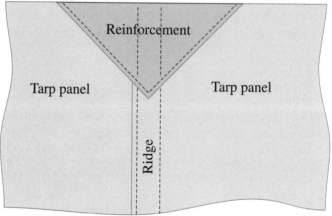

Tarp's lower surface at one end of the ridge

Double-stitch the ridge flat-felled seams through the reinforcement triangle, as shown. This is best done by turning the tarp over, and sewing along the two existing rows of stitching.

Now repeat the procedure, sewing the other reinforcement triangle to the opposite end of the ridge.

Note that for clarity, the reinforcement patch is not shown in the remaining illustrations.

Beak Construction

In a previous chapter you cut out four beak triangles. Position two of these triangles as shown. If using urethane-nylon, insure that the uncoated (less shiny) sides are together.

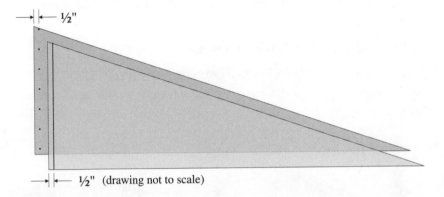

—→| |←— ½" (drawing not to scale)

You will sew these two pieces together using a flat-felled seam ½" wide as usual. Mark the two triangles, then pin them together while insuring that their base edges are aligned with each other.

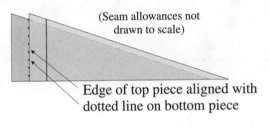

(Seam allowances not drawn to scale)

Edge of top piece aligned with dotted line on bottom piece

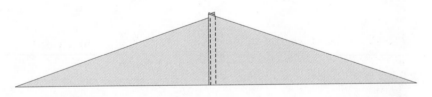

Then sew the two pieces together, and complete the flat-felled seam.

Trim the excess seam allowance protruding above the beak's apex.

Make a second beak in the same way.

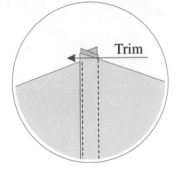

Trim

Sewing beaks to tarp

In this section you will attach the beaks to the tarp, one at each end, using the flat-felled seam.

Begin by spreading one of the beaks on the floor, with its lower surface facing down. That is, with the small fold of its flat-felled seam against the floor.

Spread the tarp nearby, with its lower surface facing up.

Position the tarp on top of the beak, as shown.

Now rotate the beak to orient its right-hand edge parallel to the top of the corresponding tarp panel.

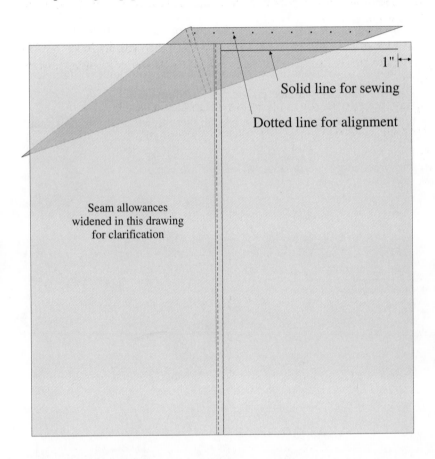

Solid line for sewing

Dotted line for alignment

Seam allowances
widened in this drawing
for clarification

Marking the pieces

Mark both the beak and panel for a flat-felled seam. The beak, on the bottom of the two-layer stack, gets a dotted line ½" from its edge. The tarp panel, on top, gets a solid line ½" from its edge. Start this line next to the ridge, and stop it 1" from the panel's right side.

In a similar fashion, mark the tarp's left-hand panel and the beak's left-hand triangle. Note that I have omitted these left-hand lines from the illustrations, for simplification.

Aligning the pieces

Align the tarp panel's upper edge with the beak's dotted line. ①

The crossover point is where the right edge of the tarp's flat-felled ridge seam crosses the right edge of the beak's flat-felled seam.

Slide the tarp to the right or left, to align the crossover point with the left-hand end of the tarp panel's sewing line, as shown. ②

With the two pieces properly aligned, pin them together along their seam allowance.

Before proceeding, verify that ① and ② are correct.

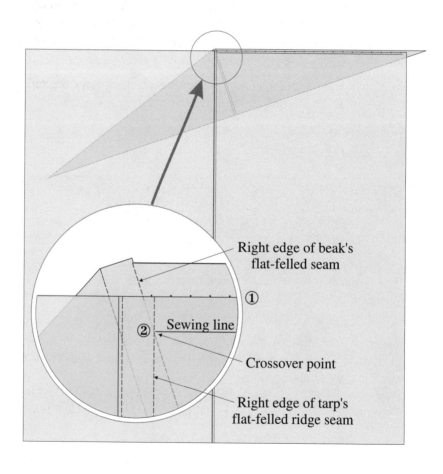

Right edge of beak's
flat-felled seam

①

② Sewing line

Crossover point

Right edge of tarp's
flat-felled ridge seam

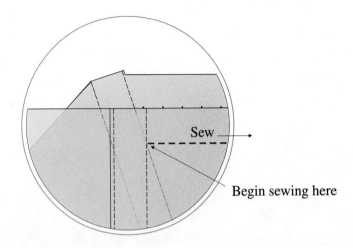

Place the project at the sewing machine, and turn the hand wheel to slowly lower the needle. The needle should penetrate the fabric layers at the leftmost end of the sewing line, but about 1/16" from the flat-felled ridge seam.

Sew the two pieces together along the line, backstitching at the beginning, and stopping about 2" from the right edge of the tarp panel.

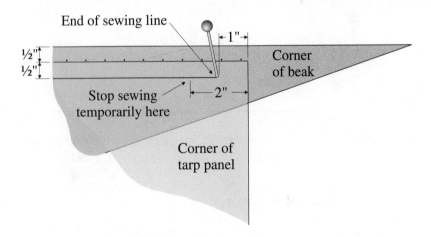

At the end of the sewing line, 1" from the panel edge, press a pin straight down through both layers to mark that point on the beak. Then remove the pin.

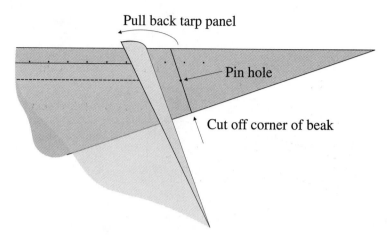

Pull back tarp panel

Pin hole

Cut off corner of beak

Peel back the tarp panel, and draw a line perpendicular to the beak's lower edge, and running through the pin hole.

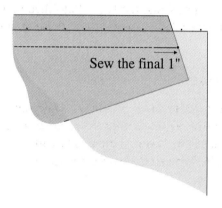

Sew the final 1"

With scissors, cut along this line, trimming the corner of the beak.

Sew the final inch along the sewing line.

Do not complete the flat-felled seam yet. Instead, repeat the instructions to join the tarp's left-hand panel to its corresponding beak triangle.

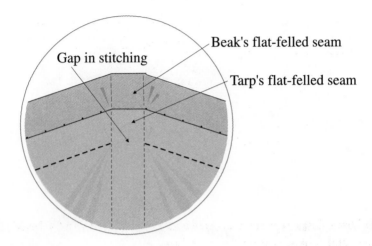

Note: do not extend either of these seams into the tarp's flat-felled seam and the beak's flat-felled seam. Leave a ½" un-sewn gap at these seams, as shown.

Complete the flat-felled seam

At this point you have sewn the beak to the tarp with a single row of stitching, and have left the ½" gap in the center. Now go ahead and complete the flat-felled seam joining tarp to beak, starting near the middle and sewing outwards each time. But here again, leave the ½" gap at the ridge.

Attach the other beak

Sew the second beak to the tarp's opposite end, using the same methods.

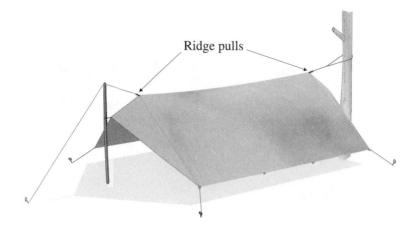

Ridge pulls

Installing the ridge pulls

The ridge pulls are short loops of nylon webbing, one sewn to each end of the ridge. The ridge guys attach to these ridge pulls.

As shown in the illustration, the tarp hangs from its ridge pulls; thus, these pulls take the greatest stress. Think of stress, for a moment, as water running through a pipe. In this case, the pipe is the tarp's ridge seam. The stress runs from one ridge guy, through the pull, through the ridge seam to the opposite ridge pull, and to its guy. This is the reason we use a flat-felled seam for the ridgeline. Being four layers thick and ½" wide, it is well suited to handle the stress.

To make the ridge pulls, cut two pieces of ½" webbing 9½" long. Lightly sear the ends with a lighter or candle flame. Caution: completely melting the webbing can create sharp edges that could later damage the tarp fabric.

You will insert the webbing through the half-inch gap, such that a part of the webbing will extend outside the tarp (to form the ridge pull loop), and a part will extend into the tarp's interior, (to form the net-tent or clothesline attachment loop). The first step is to sew a 1" loop in the webbing, prior to inserting the webbing into the gap.

Mark a piece of webbing 2" from one end, fold to create the 1" loop, and sew the loop closed. This loop will serve as an attachment point for a net-tent or clothesline.

←— 1" —→

To sew the loop closed, make three parallel rows of stitching close to the end of the webbing. With each row, stitch back and forth 3 or 4 times. A narrow zigzag stitch also works well for this, if your machine has this feature.

At one end of the tarp, insert the webbing through the gap in the beak-to-tarp seam, such that the webbing enters the seam on the tarp's lower surface, and exits the seam on the beak's upper surface. The loop in the webbing is now beneath the tarp, with its raw edge facing downward. To facilitate feeding the webbing through the gap, work the seam part way open with a pencil, before gently pushing the webbing through. If the webbing will not fit through the gap and lie flat, you may have to use a seam ripper to widen the gap a short ways to either side. This seam ripping would not affect the tarp's strength, because you will be sewing the gap closed shortly. But not yet.

Working now at the topside of the tarp and beak, pull the webbing a ways out the gap, and sew a 1½" loop in the end of the webbing, with its raw edge facing up.

Slide the webbing into the gap, leaving ¼" between the end of the loop and the beginning of the tarp's ridge, as shown.

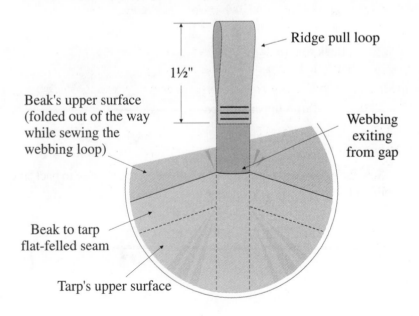

Ridge pull loop

1½"

Beak's upper surface (folded out of the way while sewing the webbing loop)

Webbing exiting from gap

Beak to tarp flat-felled seam

Tarp's upper surface

Ridge pull loop

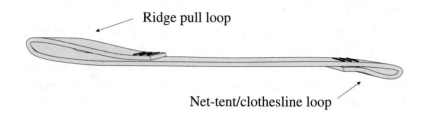

Net-tent/clothesline loop

Without the tarp and beak, the ridge pull
loop would look something like this.

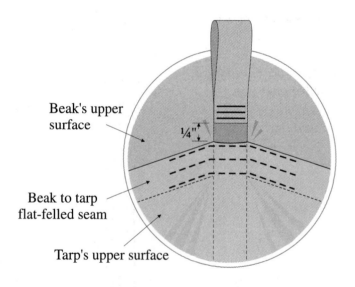

Beak's upper
surface

¼"

Beak to tarp
flat-felled seam

Tarp's upper surface

Sew the gap closed with three rows of stitching. Be sure to backstitch
at both ends of each row.

Turn the tarp over, underside up, and sew the webbing to the tarp with four parallel rows of stitching, double-stitching each row.

Important: The flat-felled ridge seam is about ½" wide, as is the ridge pull loop webbing. When sewing the webbing to the ridge, be sure to sew the webbing only to the ridge, not to the tarp body. Any stitching through the webbing that falls outside the ridge, onto the single-layer fabric, must be removed as it could later tear the tarp in a strong wind.

To double-stitch a row, sew the row start to finish, and at its end leave the needle in its down position, raise the presser foot, turn the work

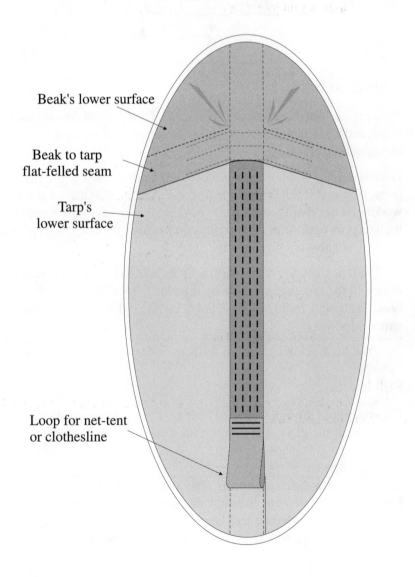

Beak's lower surface

Beak to tarp
flat-felled seam

Tarp's
lower surface

Loop for net-tent
or clothesline

180 degrees, lower the presser foot, and sew the same row a second time, directly on top of the initial row of stitching.

You have completed this ridge pull loop. Now repeat the procedure for the other pull loop at the tarp's opposite end.

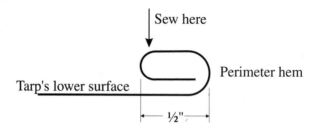

Perimeter hem

The next step is to hem the tarp's perimeter. The hem will envelop the raw edges, and it will reinforce the edges while providing a platform for sewing the remaining pull loops.

Fold the fabric ½" from its edge, toward the tarp's lower surface. Finger press, fold again, finger press, and sew. Proceed a few inches at a time, working at the sewing machine. If you find it necessary, pin or paperclip the hem prior to sewing it. And make sure you have folded the hem beneath the tarp, not above where it would catch rain.

Start at the apex of one of the beaks and work toward one corner. Return to the apex and work to the opposite corner. Repeat for the other beak. With both beaks fully hemmed, continue the process to hem the tarp's sides.

You need not double-stitch the hem; a single pass will do nicely.

Pull loops

I have designed the pull loops and their method of attachment to distribute the stress of the guys. Therefore, proper construction is essential. Done correctly the pull loops are easily done. But do not be tempted to take shortcuts. The last thing you want is your pull loops ripping off the tarp in the middle of a dark and stormy night. At the same time, you need not overbuild your pulls. The hallmark of a professionally constructed tarp is a nice set of properly constructed pulls. So take advantage of my many years of experience with tarps, and proceed with these instructions step at a time.

And please note that you will sew the pull loops to hems or flat-felled seams only, not to single-layer fabric.

In the illustration, the circles with letters represent the various pull loops, and indicate their locations.

Begin by cutting 14 pieces of half-inch webbing, each measuring 2½" in length. Lightly sear the ends of each piece.

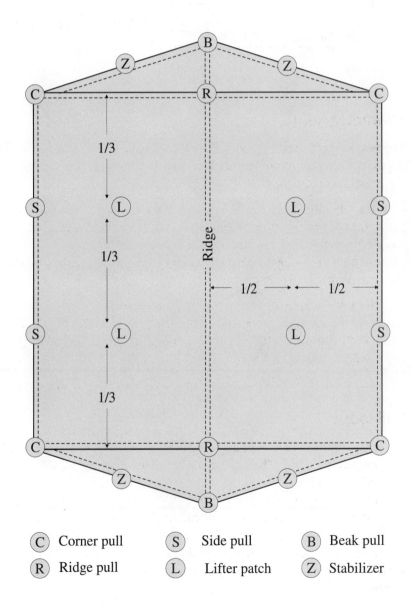

C — Corner pull   S — Side pull   B — Beak pull

R — Ridge pull   L — Lifter patch   Z — Stabilizer

Corner pull loops

Each of the tarp's four corners gets a pull loop. Select four 2½" pieces of webbing, and fold them in half as shown. Then sew them to the underside of the tarp, one end to the side hem and the other to the tarp-to-beak flat-felled seam.

Sew two parallel lines of straight stitching at each web end, each line triple-stitched and backstitched. Then sew one line of triple-stitching across both web ends, as shown.

Alternatively, you could use a zigzag stitch for these, if your machine has that capability. Either way, be careful not to sew on the single-layer tarp fabric.

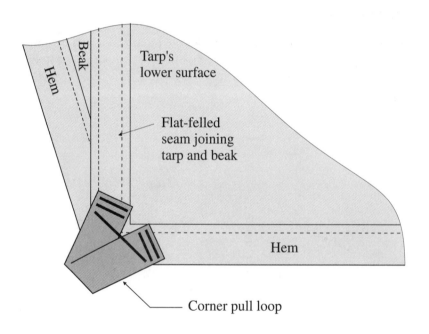

Beak

Hem

Tarp's lower surface

Flat-felled seam joining tarp and beak

Hem

Corner pull loop

Side and beak pull loops

The remaining pull loops are even easier, since they receive only two rows of stitching per web. Refer to the illustration for placement of the 4 side pulls, 4 beak stabilizer pulls, and the 2 beak tip pulls. Remember to sew all these to the tarp or beak's lower surface.

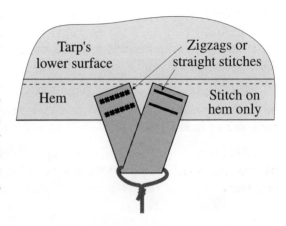

Lifter patches

See the illustration for the location of the lifter patches. By pulling upward from these patches, you raise the roof of the tarp, creating more headroom. Each half of the tarp (panel) has two lifter patches sewn directly to the fabric.

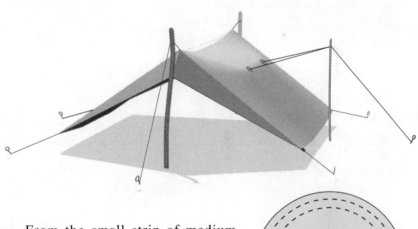

From the small strip of medium weight, coated material included in the ray-way tarp kit, cut four circular patches, each 2 inches in diameter. In each circle, cut a pair of parallel slits, ¾" long and ½" apart. These slits create a loop into which the lifter yoke (cord) attaches.

With the flame of a lighter or candle, lightly sear all edges to help prevent raveling and fraying. The material is coated, so this searing can be very lightly done.

One option is to make buttonholes rather than cutting slits, if your sewing machine can make them.

Another option is to make your lifter patches square or octagonal rather than round. I prefer round patches because they spread the load more evenly, so are much less likely to tear the tarp fabric in a strong blow or snow load.

Now sew each lifter patch to the tarp, making two concentric rows of stitching around the patch's perimeter. Work slowly, sewing only a few stitches at a time. And stop the needle in the down position whenever you need to turn the piece.

Utility loops

A pair of utility loops beneath each end of the tarp (four altogether) can be quite useful for hanging small items that you may want close at hand but out of harm's way. These might include eyeglasses, flashlight, and perhaps an alarm-type wristwatch suspended overhead where you might be more likely to hear it than if worn on the wrist.

To make the utility loops, cut four pieces of webbing 2" long. Sew these to the beak-to-body flat-felled seams on the tarp's lower surface, midway between ridge and corner, one on each side. The tarp gets two loops at one end, and two loops at the other end. At each end of the webbing sew two rows of stitching, double-stitch and backstitch. And again, sew only to the flat-felled seam, avoiding the single layer tarp or beak fabric.

Attaching the guys

The sewing is complete, and the tarp project is nearly finished. At this point you will cut the guys to length and tie them to their pull loops. This is easily accomplished, using the line supplied in the tarp kit. If the kit contains more than one type of line, refer to the instructions in the kit, as to which type of line goes where.

A couple of general notes:

• After cutting braided cord, sear its ends lightly to prevent raveling.

• Attach all guys to their pulls with an overhand on a bight.

Ridge guys

Cut two 10-foot pieces of cord, and tie one to each ridge pull loop. The 10-foot length is quite generous, but necessary when using support sticks, as it allows the two stakes to be placed with sufficient separation. It also enables the use of trees that are fairly wide in diameter, or that are spaced substantially farther apart than the tarp is long.

Corner guys

Cut four corner guys 4½ feet each, and tie to the corner pull loops.

Side guys

Cut four pieces 3½ feet in length, and tie them to the side guys.

Beak guys

Cut two pieces of line 3 feet each. Tie one to each beak pull loop. This is the loop at the apex of each beak.

Lifters: yoke and guy

Cut two lifter yokes (lines) 5½ feet each. Also cut two lifter guys 8 feet each.

Tie the yoke to the lifter patches with overhand on a bite knots.

Note: You have already learned how to tie this knot at one end of a line. To tie it at the other end, tie an overhand near that free end, feed the free end through the lifter patch slot, then feed the end back through the overhand.

Midway along the yoke, attach a lifter guy with a taut-line hitch. This is a friction knot, preventing the guy from sliding back and forth along the yoke too freely. In the field you can tie the lifter guy to a branch of an overhead tree. Or run it laterally up and out to a lifter support stick, then down to a stake.

Clothesline

Finally, cut 10 feet of line for the clothesline. Use taut-line hitches at both ends. Tension the line only enough to prevent excessive sagging. Avoid over tensioning, as this would distort the pitch.

Beak stabilizer lines

The tarp kit does not contain line for the beak stabilizers. This is because they are rarely used, only in very high wind. Carry extra cord for use around camp, and use some of this as beak stabilizer line if needed.

The sewing is complete and you are almost ready to go camping! One more item on the agenda: sealing the seams.

Seam Sealing

If your tarp is silicone-nylon, seal its seams with clear 100% silicone sealant. This is available at home improvement and hardware stores. Note that all 100% silicone sealants (GE Silicone II, auto/marine, etc) are essentially the same thing.

If your tarp is urethane-nylon, use Seam Grip or AquaSeal, both from the McNett Corporation. These two products work especially well when mixed with their accelerators. The accelerator strengthens the compound somewhat, and greatly shortens cure time.

Apply these compounds outdoors, never indoors where the fumes could accumulate and affect your health. Even outdoors, avoid breathing the fumes. And work only in 10 or 15 minute intervals, allowing your respiratory system to recover and the compound's solvents to evaporate. The idea is to split the job into short sessions, allowing one or two hours' drying time in between.

And be very careful not to glob on the sealant thickly. Feel the weight of the tube of sealant in your hand. That is the weight you would add to your tarp were you to apply the sealant indiscriminately.

To begin, pitch the tarp very tightly on a clear, windless day, preferably in an area free of dust. The taut pitch helps spread the seams and encourages the sealant to penetrate them a little better. Then clean the seams using a clean cotton cloth dampened with a mild degreasing solvent such as rubbing or denatured alcohol. This will remove any manufacturing residue, sewing machine oil, and skin oil, and will help the sealant bond to the fabric and stitching. After cleaning, allow the tarp to dry for at least an hour before applying the sealant.

With silicone sealant, apply a small dab to your fingertip, then rub the compound back and forth, pressing it into the seam. With Seam Grip or AquaSeal, do the same with a small, stiff brush. Build it very slightly on the stitching, and overlap it a quarter inch on both sides. Then wipe the overlap—the part not covering the actual stitching—as thinly as possible.

Which seams to seal

On the tarp's upper surface, seal the ridge pull loop, top and bottom where it enters the tarp. Still working on the tarp's upper surface, seal the flat-felled seams of the tarp and beaks, and the stitching of the triangular reinforcement patches.

Now on the tarp's lower surface, seal only the lifter patches stitching.

Do not seal the hems or their pull loops, top or bottom, as this would only add weight while serving no useful purpose.

Seam seal the stowbags also, on their outsides only. First, load them tightly with rags or whatever, to stretch the seams.

After each sealing session, remove any sealant from your skin with a paper towel, then wash with hot, soapy water.

When finished, allow the sealant to cure undisturbed for a day or two.

Finally, test your seam sealing with a garden hose. Ask someone to hose the tarp as you crouch inside looking for leaks. Be aware, however, that on a humid day the cold water from a hose can induce condensation to form on the tarp's inner surface, making the tarp appear to be leaking. Look carefully for beads of water actually coming through the seams.

Care of your tarp

Silicone-nylon and urethane-nylon are surprisingly durable fabrics, when well cared for. Here are a few guidelines:

• Be careful not to step on the tarp while making or breaking camp.

• Avoid pitching the tarp in contact with a tree, branches, rocks, or anything that might abrade holes should the wind pick up.

• Keep the tarp well away from a campfire where an eruption of sparks could burn holes. Also remember that these lightweight materials are flammable.

• Pitching the tarp in the sun is fine, but do not leave it in the sun needlessly day after day.

• To store the tarp between seasons, dry it thoroughly then place in its stowbag.

Repairs

Should the tarp become punctured, torn or abraded, here is how you can easily repair it:

For quick, temporary repairs to urethane-nylon, use duct tape. Alternatively, tape the tear closed from the underside, apply sealant to the upper side, then after the sealant has cured, remove the tape. To repair more extensive damage, sew a patch to the tarp's upper surface, and still working on the upper surface, seam seal the stitching and the perimeter of the patch.

Adhesive tape does not adhere well to silicone-nylon. For this material, repair very small holes and small areas of abrasion with silicone sealant, rubbing it in with a fingertip. For larger areas, sew a silicone-nylon patch to the tarp's upper surface, and seam seal as described above.

Optional gear pocket

A small gear pocket might be useful for containing beak stabilizer lines and extra guys. It would hang from the flat-felled seam between tarp and beak, near the ridge. If you would like to make one, keep it very small and simple. Use scraps from your tarp kit, and make the bag similar to the stowbags, but without the draw cord and casing. More specifically, cut a rectangle 12 inches by 4 inches. Hem the two short ends first, then sew the two side seams. Turn the pocket right side out, then sew the hem on one side of the pocket to the tarp's flat-felled seam.

Congratulations!

You have finished making your tarp and stowbags, and can be very proud of them. Now it is time to go try them out. I am sure you will find, as I have, that camping beneath your home-made tarp is a richly satisfying experience, and one that you can enjoy night after night, for many years to come.

Non recommended options

• What about omitting the beaks, and simply making the ridge that much longer than the sides? Answer: This would produce "beaks" that do not droop. Such beaks would add very little protection when the tarp is pitched low-lying in a storm.

• What about omitting the beak seams and simply notching the material at each end, and sewing the notches together to create beaks? Answer: This would not be a good idea, because the beak-to-tarp seams are structural, in that they carry much of the stress between the corner and ridge guys. Without these seams, a large stress riser would exist at each ridge pull loop, and if these areas were not heavily reinforced, they could tear out during a storm.

• What about adding false seams? Answer: False seams along what would be the beak-to-tarp seams might carry the stress well, as long as they connect properly to the ridge pulls, and are reinforced in that area. However, the extra time and effort spent measuring and laying out the odd-shaped panel pieces, and figuring out how to sew everything together, would unlikely justify the results. And why bother, when sewing the beaks to the tarp with the flat-felled seam is easy and effective?

• What about using a French seam for the ridge and beak-to-tarp seams? Answer: To create a French seam, one sews two layers of material together leaving a small seam allowance, turns the two layers inside out, such that the seam allowance is now on the inside, then runs another line of stitching a certain ways from the first one. The French seam is weaker than the flat-felled because only one row of stitching carries the stress. With the flat-felled seam, both rows of stitching share the stress, and because they are separated by half an inch, they help distribute that stress throughout the individual fibers of material.

Sewing a Net-Tent

The net-tent is a netting enclosure that fits beneath the ray-way tarp. It is shaped like a miniature wall tent, with a floor, gabled roof, and a wall on each of its four sides. It consists of only five pieces, sewn together very simply. Anyone who has made a ray-way tarp can easily construct a net-tent to go along with it.

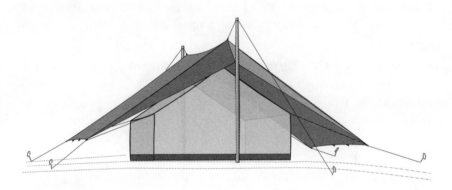

The net-tent kit

The net-tent kit, from Ray-Way Products, contains all the needed materials for a two-person net-tent, or a one-person model. This includes no-see-um netting for the roof and walls, silicone-nylon for the floor, suspension lines, reinforcement material, cord locks, and attachment hooks. Also included is an extra cord lock for a net-tent stowbag, which you can make from excess floor material.

Project overview

1. The process will begin with cutting the netting pieces to size.

2. These netting pieces you will sew together. Then you will:

3. Add reinforcement patches,

4. Cut out the silicone-nylon floor, and make a perimeter rim,

5. Sew the floor to the netting walls,

6. And to complete the project you will fit the attachment lines, hooks and cord locks.

Cutting the netting pieces

The Cutting Layout, shown here, illustrates the sizes of the netting pieces, depending on whether you are making a two-person net-tent or a one-person model. Each model has a pair of side/roof panels, a headwall, and a footwall. All dimensions shown in the diagram include the seam allowances.

To mark a piece of dark-colored netting prior to cutting it, apply a short strip of masking or clear adhesive tape in the estimated location, then mark the tape with a permanent marker. After cutting, remove the tape.

Roof/side panels

Begin by marking and cutting a pair of roof/side panels. The two panels are identical. Each one comprises half the roof and its adjacent sidewall. In other words, the net-tent has no seam between roof and sidewall. But it will have a ridge seam, after you have sewn the two panels together.

For a two-person net-tent, each panel is 82 inches long and 44 inches wide. (Panels for a one-person net-tent are 82" x 33".)

Cutting Layout
No-see-um netting

Two-person Net-Tent

One-person Net-Tent

Roof/side panel 2-person

82"

44"

Roof/side panel 2-person

82"

44"

Headwall 2-person

43"

50"

Footwall 2-person

31"

50"

Roof/side panel 1-person

82"

33"

Roof/side panel 1-person

82"

33"

Headwall 1-person

37"

32"

Footwall 1-person

25"

32"

Headwall and Footwall Dimensions

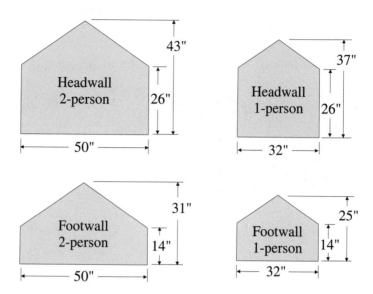

Headwall and Footwall

The illustration shows the headwall and footwall for the two-person and one-person net-tents. Begin by cutting out the two rectangles, one for the headwall and one the footwall. Then referring to the dimensions given in the illustration, cut the roof slope. To locate the apex on a rectangular piece of material, fold the piece in half along its top edge, then mark the fold. Be sure to check your measurements before cutting, to insure that you have the piece oriented correctly and not rotated 90 degrees.

Sewing the ridge seam

You will sew the pair of roof/side panels together along their length, using a flat-felled seam. Mark and pin the pieces, then go ahead and sew the seam. The seam is 82" long, and will become the net-tent's ridge.

Note that the netting does not have a "right side" or a "wrong side." The small fold of the flat-felled seams can go inside the enclosure or outside.

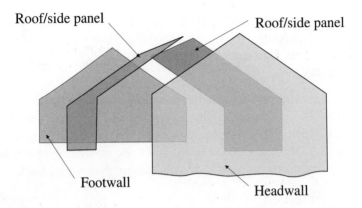

Roof/side panel   Roof/side panel

Footwall   Headwall

Sew the footwall to the roof/side panels

Next: mark, pin and sew the footwall to the side/roof panels, again with the flat-felled seam. Begin at the ridge, and sew to one lower corner. Then return to the ridge and sew to the opposite lower corner.

After you have sewn these seams, you might find that one piece of netting is somewhat longer than the other. Simply trim the excess by cutting off a long and very narrow triangle, as guided by a yardstick.

Attach the headwall

Sew the headwall to the side/roof panels in the same way. Note that the headwall extends 12 inches below the bottom of the sidewalls, to form the door flap. Thus, the flat-felled seam extends from the apex, down the roof on either side, and down the sidewall to its bottom edge, leaving the extension flap free.

Reinforcement patches

The net-tent will connect to the tarp with lines and hooks. Each line will hook to the tarp in the appropriate place, lead to the net-tent, pass through a tiny hole in the netting, then to an adjustable cord lock within the net-tent's interior. The hole must be protected from the sawing action of the line, not with a small grommet, which would allow entry to miniscule insects, but with a simple, circular reinforcement patch with an equally tiny hole in its center.

From the reinforcement material included with the kit, cut eight circular patches 1½" diameter. These you will sew to the net-tent at the designated locations. These patches do not require hems. And if you happen to have a glue stick, you could swipe the back of a patch and glue it temporarily to the netting prior to sewing it there permanently.

As you stitch, follow the perimeter of the patch, making a single row of stitching 1/8" from the edge.

① Sew a reinforcement patch to the ridge where it meets the footwall, centering it on the middle of the intersecting flat-felled seams.

Reinforcement patch locations

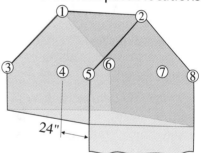

Sew this first patch to either side of the netting. That side then becomes the net-tent's designated interior. Sew the remaining patches to the interior side of the netting also.

② Sew a similar patch at the opposite end of the ridge, where it meets the headwall.

③⑤⑥⑧ Sew a patch to each corner, where the footwall or headwall makes the bend from sidewall to roof.

④⑦ Sew the "shoulder" patches 24" from the headwall, at the same 14" height as the four corner patches.

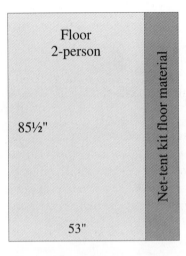

Make the floor

If making a 2-person net-tent, cut the silicone-nylon 85½" by 53" (85½" by 35" for a 1-person).

Forming the rim

The floor has a perimeter rim, 2" high, and this rim is easy to construct. Near one corner, mark 2½" from each edge and make a reference dot. Then draw a stitching line, from the dot to one edge, as shown.

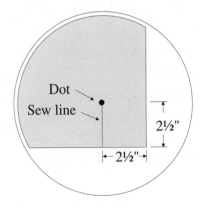

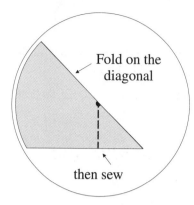

Fold on the diagonal

then sew

Fold the corner on a diagonal, bringing the edges together. Finger press the fold, and pin. Then double-stitch along the line, (two rows of stitching, one on top of the other) backstitching at each end.

Trim the corner, leaving a ¼" seam allowance.

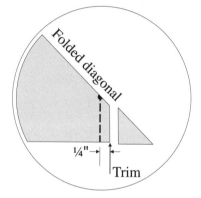

Folded diagonal

¼"→

Trim

Repeat for the other three corners of the net-tent floor, making sure that all four seam allowances face the same way, which will be toward the net-tent's interior.

Turn the floor corners right-side-out, facing the seam allowances to the inside.

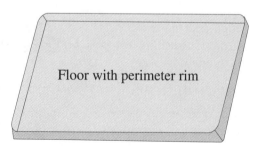

Floor with perimeter rim

Sewing the floor to the netting

The floor joins to the netting footwall and two sidewalls, but not to the headwall. The headwall is identified by its extra 12" height.

To join the sidewalls and footwall to the floor, you will use the "felled" seam.

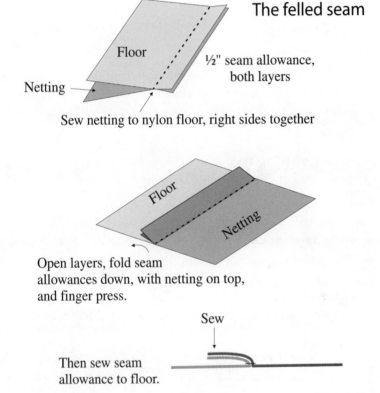

The felled seam

Floor

Netting →

½" seam allowance, both layers

Sew netting to nylon floor, right sides together

Floor

Netting

Open layers, fold seam allowances down, with netting on top, and finger press.

Sew

Then sew seam allowance to floor.

The felled seam

Sewing the felled seam is easy, but you may wish to practice on a pair of small scraps.

1. Place one piece on the other, with both sewing edges flush.

2. Pin the two pieces together and sew a line of straight stitching, leaving the usual ½" seam allowance, and backstitching at each end.

3. Spread the layers apart, fold the seam allowances down, toward the bottom piece, and finger press them down.

4. Sew a second row parallel to the first and about 3/8" from it, stitching the two seam allowances to the bottom piece. As you sew, pull the two pieces lightly apart.

Note: the no-see-um netting has a factory finish, to prevent raveling.

You will sew the floor to the sidewalls and footwall in two stages, initially joining the three netting pieces to the floor with the first seam, then going back and completing the felled seam with the second stitch.

Begin by pinning the footwall to the floor, proceeding as follows:

Find one footwall corner, and its corresponding floor corner.

(Remember to pin the pieces together with their insides facing away from each other. The reinforcement circles are on the inside of the net-tent, and the corner seam allowances are on the inside of the floor.)

Center the netting's flat-felled seam on the floor's corner seam.

Align the edge of the floor with the edge of the footwall, and pin the two pieces together at this point, inside the usual ½" seam allowance.

Note: Were you to work your way, pin by pin, to the other side of the footwall, you would likely find excess netting there. This is because the netting would have stretched slightly between each pin. Here is how to prevent this problem:

Pin the opposite corner of the footwall to the floor, centering the seams as before.

Pin the seam allowances together again, this time at the center of the footwall and floor.

Split the difference on either side of center, and pin again.

Repeat, placing pins mid-way between each span, until the pins are about 6" apart.

Now, sew the pieces together. As you sew, the netting may stretch somewhat. If this happens, take small but frequent tucks in the netting to even the excess.

With the footwall sewn to the floor, completing only the first half of the felled seam, repeat the pinning and sewing with one sidewall. Then again with the other sidewall.

Then go back and finish the felled seam by finger pressing the seam allowance to the floor material, and sewing the second row of stitching.

Suspension lines

The net-tent secures to the tarp with attachment lines. The length of these lines are as follows:

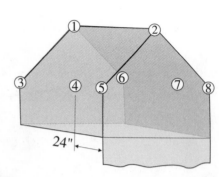

①② ridge lines: 44" in length.

③⑤⑥⑧ 4 corner lines: 44" each. (54" for 1-person model)

④⑦ 2 side lines: 34" each. (44" for 1-person)

Melt the ends of each line lightly to prevent fraying.

Tie a hook to one end of each line, using an overhand on a bight.

Sharpen the opposite end of each line, by melting its end and quickly shaping it into a needle-point by pinching and drawing it repeatedly through a rag or paper towel held between thumb and index finger. Use caution to avoid touching the hot polyester with a finger.

Using an ice pick or nail, punch a small hole through the center of each suspension line reinforcement patch and its adjacent netting seam. Ideally, the ice pick or nail would spread the material threads apart rather than actually cutting them.

Working on the outside surface of the net-tent, locate the circular patch at ① at the headwall apex. Pass the sharpened end of one ridge suspension line through the hole in the netting, and through the corresponding hole in the reinforcement patch. If the line will not feed through the holes, re-melt and sharpen its tip, and perhaps widen the holes somewhat. But keep the holes as small as possible, to prevent bugs entering.

Pull the line through the hole, such that half the line is inside the net-tent, and half is outside.

Repeat for the remaining suspension lines.

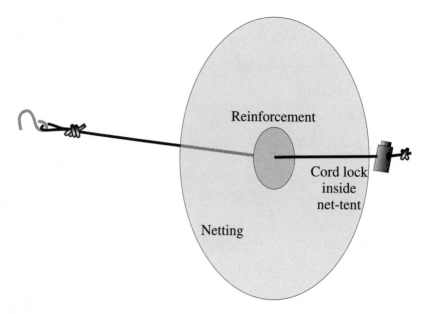

Installing cord locks

A typical attachment line is shown in the illustration. Inside the net-tent, the line passes through a cord lock, and is terminated with a "keeper knot." The keeper knot, an overhand on a bight, prevents the loss of the cord lock. Position this knot about an inch from the end of the line.

The cord lock enables you to adjust the net-tent's shape from within its protected interior. This adjustment is necessary because of the tarp's variable geometry.

Sewing a stowbag for the net-tent

Construct a net-tent stowbag using silicone-nylon left over from the floor. Make it the same size as your tarp stowbag, and follow the same sewing procedures.

The left over netting could be used for small, see-through ditty bags, or bug-protective items like head nets, booties, and mitts.

Seam seal the floor corners

Seam sealing the floor's corner seams is optional, but easily done since each seam is only 2" in length, and there are only four of them. Apply the sealant to the outside of the seams. You need not pitch the net-tent to accomplish this.

For instructions on attaching the net-tent to the tarp, refer to the net-tent chapter, earlier in this book.

Congratulations on a job well done! It's time to go camping and try out your new net-tent.

A few sewing options

You could make the floor rim taller, from 2" to, say 6" or even 12". At least on the sides and foot. This would help the rim stand up, and create a type of "bathtub" floor. Personally, I do not find this type of floor necessary.

You could add a zippered door if you like. This would avoid the need to crawl through the bottom slot. But it would also add the weight, complexity and the vulnerability of the zippers.

You could make your net-tent wider and/or longer to suit. The dimensions given in this chapter are meant to provide sufficient room for most people, while minimizing the net-tent's weight. Should you choose a different size, draw it on paper to scale, then measure the size of the pieces.

You could taper the net-tent's floor plan, making it narrower at the foot. This would require a narrower footwall, a seam between sidewall and roof, and tapered roof panels.

You could give the net-tent a sloped profile, making it shorter at the foot. This would require the similar modifications as above. It would also necessitate the tarp be sloped in the same way. This is because the net-tent's ridge must parallel the tarp's ridge. Otherwise, when tensioning the net-tent, you would lift its foot area off the ground.

My recommendation is to keep it simple. Make it rectangular and zipper free, and enjoy.

Origins of the Term Ray-Way

The "Ray Way" refers to Ray Jardine's style of adventuring. While Ray has built his reputation in several fields, the backpacking community originated this term.

In 1987, Ray and Jenny Jardine hiked the Pacific Crest Trail in 4½ months, using conventional backpacking equipment. They discovered that only 5% of aspiring thru-hikers completed the trail and that less than 20% finished the first 100 miles. Ray and Jenny modified their hiking style and completed their second thru-hike of the PCT in 1991. Subsequently, Ray wrote the first edition of The PCT Hiker's Handbook, which appeared in 1992 and elicited a response of about 2,500 letters.

In 1993, Scott Williamson and his friends coined the "Ray Way" term during their thru-hike of the Pacific Crest Trail. He wrote, "Along the way I met other thru-hikers, and was surprised to find most of them were also following many, if not all, of the Handbook's methods. What a change from the previous year when everyone had heavy packs and boots. Now, all but a very few carried much lighter packs and wore running shoes. We talked constantly about various aspects of the 'Ray Way,' as we called it."

While the "Ray Way" term did not always appear in early interviews and book reviews, it continued to circulate among hikers. At the front of The PCT Hiker's Handbook, Second Edition 1996, this quote by Anders Åhnberg appears: "My congratulations for an excellent book. The 'Ray Way' is starting in Sweden too."

In December 1996 a book review of The PCT Hiker's Handbook, second edition appeared in Backpacker magazine. By this time, Ray and Jenny had hiked the PCT for the third time, averaging over 28 miles of walking per day. Mark Jenkins wrote, "Once every two or three decades a book comes along that fundamentally reshapes how we think. Jardine's PCT Hiker's Handbook is such a work... It could change your hiking life."

The February 1998 issue of Backpacker emblazoned the "Ray Way" in the headline of an article. In that article, Peter Potterfield wrote: "In 1994 Ray and Jenny hiked the PCT a third time, covering the 2,700 miles in only three months and four days-almost 45 days quicker than the first time. They didn't walk any faster, they just spent more hours each day on the trail... And thus was born The Ray Way, a blend of philosophy and innovative techniques culled from the hard lessons learned while hiking more than 12,000 total miles." Actually, Ray has hiked more than 20,000 miles.

After the Backpacker article, the "Ray Way" term entered common use among hikers and in print. Ray used the Potterfield quote on the back cover of Beyond Backpacking, which he published in 2000. But he did not use the term in the book itself. Nevertheless, in this book Ray explains how his style evolved from conventional to ultralight equipment over five megahikes. And he describes his current equipment, much of which is his own invention. So it is with a certain inevitability that "Ray Way" has come to signify this gear as well, and is now the defining term for the tarp of Ray's design.

- Charles Duane, Brett Tucker

Testimonials

Doug A.: *Wonderful philosophy and incredible experiences--a few lifetimes worth for most folks! Tried out your tarp and net-tent in heavy rain and wind out in Anza-Borrego. Super design. Thanks for the equipment design and thoughts.*

Philip C.: *I made your tarp over the weekend. The whole project went very well considering I'd never used a sewing machine before. I left the tarp up over the weekend in windy and rainy New Zealand and it worked very well. A couple of the neighborhood cats took up residence in it for a while so it must be good. Thanks very much for a great project.*

Brian B.: *Just wanted to let you know that I finished a tarp based on your specifications. Sewing got much easier as the project progressed and I imagine my next project will be even better. The tarp worked well on a very wet trip this weekend to the Mt. Mitchell area of North Carolina. Setup really is no problem. I think my fiancée is beginning to see the light. We incorporated a lot of your ideas on this trip. The light packs and running sneakers made the tough terrain seem easier.*

Jack H.: *Impressive, inspirational books. Thanks to your sound evolutionary engineering and willingness to share, I've just completed a tarp and quilt. Thanks so much for sharing and caring about others.*

David M.: *I finished the tarp today, and I can't wait for the seam sealer to set up. A lot of the time, I will use it for canoe camping, and so can use a couple of paddles for the main supports.*

Karen: *I just returned from Montana's Glacier National Park where I used my newly made tarp, net-tent, and pack. My husband kept his traditional gear but agreed to leave the tent and use my new stuff. We both loved it! We had a fantastic trip and a few people we camped with were curious about my homemade gear. And with a 20 pound pack I had much more fun than my last trip to Glacier where I carried 50 pounds. Thanks for the great ideas.*

Nickolas G.: *I constructed the tarp according to your instructions. It worked marvelously, both in high winds and substantial rain during a kayaking trip. I think this was the first time on the northwest coast of British Columbia that I have ever been totally dry and condensation free in the rain. Thanks!*

Tom J.: *I just finished a thru-hike of the John Muir Trail in 15 days. I am 46 years old. I could not have done the hike without the "Ray Way" and equipment. Thank you for giving me the knowledge and the methods to complete the journey.*

David S.: *Thank you for all the help you've been to me. After reading Beyond Backpacking, I sewed my own quilt, tarp and net-tent. My approach to backpacking has changed for the better, and I want you to know I appreciate your part in it.*

Gordon: *I just yesterday finished the net tent and tarp projects and was writing to tell you thanks for the advice and reassurance you've given. The directions were right on and clearly laid out. Your efforts have made a big difference for me. I had contemplated making a home-made tarp. Now, I've done it. I've thought about making clothing to get away from the highly marketed and "logoed" commercial stuff. Now, I have confidence to do it. Suffice it to say that your books and web site have provided me with inspiration. Particularly because you seem to have done all this in a way that's all about enjoying the beauties of nature and realizing goals and attributes people already have inside them.*

Charlie D.: *One-person tarp completed. The project has taken maybe two weekends. Without lines, stakes, seam sealing, and stowbag, the tarp weighs 10.5 ounces. Thanks for challenging me to learn a new skill, and also for supplying the tarp design.*

Jake S.: *Just got your book and read it. Love the concept and the tarp worked great during a huge Alabama rain storm.*

Kirsten M.: *My husband received your latest book for his birthday. On a recent weekend snowshoeing trip in the El Dorado National Forest we had a chance to try a poly-tarp instead of our tent. We had a sturdy, spacious comfortable shelter in only 15 minutes. Not bad for a first try! Now I'd like to surprise him with a sewn tarp.*

Steven: *Finished sewing your tarp project today, I really enjoyed the project and can't wait to try it out! Have found your books educational, entertaining and inspiring! Thank you for sharing!*

Joe G.: *I think the hardest part about the ultralite concept is shifting the paradigm from what you THINK you need to what you REALLY need. I think the outdoor gear market is going to change for the better as a result of your contributions and I look forward to your next projects!*

Klondike: *I finished the two person silicone nylon tarp. My wife was impressed with my new sewing skills.*

Joe H.: *Last September my wife Buttercup and I were sitting at a camp site in the Sierras after lugg'n my 65 and her 45 lb pack up 2000 ft for 10 miles. I was staring at my swollen knee wondering what I could possibly do to lighten my load. I couldn't think of anything. We came across another hiker that was carrying a 30 lb pack and he told us about "Beyond Backpacking." Three months later I had knee surgery and spent two months in a wheelchair. Concerned about my continued prospects for hiking I purchased your book.*

I've been hiking for 40 years, and spent most of my life in the woods or on the water. I had experienced all that I read in your book, but was unable to put it together as a hiking process. You did that for me.

Last week, Buttercup and I completed a test hike on the AT. We were carrying 20 lb Ray Way packs. We had a Ray-way tarp and quilts. We wore trail running shoes. The trip was a complete success. The small amount of gear we had was all we needed. The tarp performed very well in a heavy mountain storm due to proper site selection. We enjoyed the trip more than most, not because of the trail, but primarily because the focus was on the hike and not the heavy burden of the pack. My knee tolerated the light load without difficulty.

I'm glad I ran into that disciple of lightweight backpacking that starry night, and I thank you for your words which helped me stay on the trail.

Eric: *I have read Beyond Backpacking and sewn a tarp, also a one person version, a net tent, a large quilt, two small quilts and several stuff bags. My pack now weighs much less. My wife and I will continue to enjoy nature with less on our backs. All of these changes are in large part due to your life, which has a very definite ripple effect on many more people than you will ever know. I for one would like to thank you.*

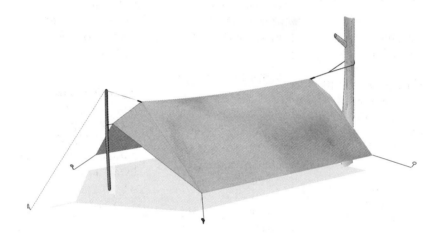

Index

Author's Profile

Ray Jardine holds a degree in Aeronautical and Astronautical Engineering from Northrop University. He worked in the aerospace industry as a specialist in computer-simulated space-flight mechanics, but retired at an early age to pursue his outdoor interests.

Ray has climbed most of Colorado's fourteeners, many in winter. He has also climbed extensively across western North America. His highest peak was Peru's Huascarán, at 22,205 feet.

A wilderness instructor, Ray worked for the Colorado Alpine Winter Mountaineering School for two seasons, and Outward Bound for seven. During these classes he accumulated several thousand backpacking miles. He also holds an EMT certificate from St. Anthony's Hospital in Denver, Colorado.

A rock climber, Ray established some of the era's toughest climbs, including the world's first 5.12 graded climb, The Crimson Cringe, and the first 5.13, The Phoenix. He climbed extensively in Great Britain and across western America. His ascents in Colorado include seven Diamond routes. In Yosemite Valley he pioneered 50 first ascents, and was the first to free climb a grade VI. He invented the protection and anchoring device known as the "Friend," which revolutionized the sport. And he originated the style of climbing used today that enables far more challenging routes to be climbed. According to Rock & Ice magazine, "The brilliance of his routes, the undeniable contributions of his designs, and his yet-unrealized visions of the future of the sport place Ray Jardine among the rarest of climbing revolutionaries."

Retiring from climbing in the early 1980's, Ray with his wife Jenny put to sea aboard their ketch SUKA, an acronym for "Seeking UnKnown Adventures," and sailed around the world in 3½ years. Ray is also a PADI-certified scuba diver.

Ray has flown sailplanes, and has an Australian Restricted Private Pilot's License. He is also an avid hang glider pilot, having logged some 400 hours aloft, flown to 16,000 feet, cross-country 50 miles, and thermal gained 9,100 feet (nearly two miles straight up).

In 1987 the Jardines hiked from Mexico to Canada, generally along the Pacific Crest Trail in 4½ months. In 1991 they hiked the PCT again, in 3 months, 3 weeks. In 1992 they hiked the Continental Divide Trail in 3 months, 3½ weeks. In 1993, the Appalachian Trail in 2 months, 28 days. And in 1994 they hiked the PCT southbound in 3 months and 4 days. Experienced gleaned from these thousands of trail miles and hundreds of nights spent on the trails inspired Ray to write two books about long-distance hiking: *The Pacific Crest Trail Hiker's Handbook* (out of print) and *Beyond Backpacking*.

In 1999, Ray and Jenny were featured guests in the BBC television series *Wilderness Walks* with host Cameron McNeish.

Together, Ray and Jenny have sea-kayaked several thousand miles in areas such as offshore California, the Sea of Cortez, French Polynesia, Australia, Alaska and Canada. In 1988 they paddled from Anacortes, Washington 3,300 miles through the Inside Passage, over the Chilkoot trail by portage, and down the Yukon River to the Bering Sea. Continuing the summer of 1995 in a kayak of their own design and construction, they paddled another 600 miles along the rugged coast of Arctic Alaska. And the summer of 1996 they returned in yet another home-built kayak and paddled the remaining 1,400 miles to Point Barrow and across the top of Alaska to Monument 1 at the Alaska/Canada border. In 1997 they paddled 975 miles down the Mackenzie River, then 200 miles of Arctic coastline until stopped by polar pack ice. That same summer they paddled a canoe 575 miles down the remote Thelon River from Lynx Lake to the Inuit hamlet of Baker Lake near Hudson Bay. Subsequent canoe trips across the Barrenlands of Arctic Canada include the Back and Meadowbank Rivers, 730 mi., and the Kazan River, 560 miles.

Ray and Jenny are also avid skydivers, specializing in free-flying. Ray has made close to 2,600 jumps and Jenny 2,000.

The fall of 2002, Ray and Jenny rowed their 23-foot ocean rowboat "Caper" across the Atlantic Ocean from Canary Islands, Spain, to Barbados in the Caribbean. Powered only by oars, they made the 3,000 mile crossing in 53 days.

For more information about the Jardines, their videos, books, classes and kits, see www.ray-way.com or visit Ray's web site at: www.RayJardine.com. Or search for "Ray Jardine's Adventure Page"

Ray-Way Products

www.ray-way.com   email: rayway@isp01.net

P.O. Box 2153 Arizona City, AZ 85223

We invite you to visit our web site for more information about our products:

• Beyond Backpacking

First published in 1998, this book is now in its fourth printing and continues to be the leading source of information on lightweight hiking and backpacking. Written by Ray Jardine. Published by AdventureLore Press. ISBN 0-9632359-3-1. $19.95

• Atlantic Caper, the video

A fantastic, 48 minute glimpse into the world of ocean rowing, chronicling Ray and Jenny's Atlantic crossing. From sea trials, training and gear preparations to the boat's launching, provisioning and departure day, this video shows what it takes to make a trip of this magnitude become reality. The actual footage at sea, the mid-ocean close-encounters with freighters, the sometimes rough motion, the rolling, flying spray, calm sunsets... will put you right there on the rowing seat.

This video captures the determination and thrill of crossing an ocean in a small rowboat, and the joy of a successful landfall after 3,000 miles and 53 days. Produced by Ray Jardine, 2003. Available in NTSC or PAL formats.

NTSC – $15.95

PAL (European format) – $19.95

• The Ray-Way Tarp Book

Written by Ray Jardine and published in 2003 by AdventureLore Press. ISBN 0-9632359-5-8. $14.95

• Ray-Way Tarp and Net-tent Kits

These two kits mark the start of the ray-way line of sew-your-own outdoor gear and clothing. They contain all the materials needed to sew your own Ray-Way Tarp and Net-tent. Check www.ray-way.com for prices and additional kits as they become available.